OCCULT SCIENCE

IN

MEDICINE

BY

FRANZ HARTMANN, M.D.

DEDICATED
TO EVERY STUDENT OF MEDICINE

"That which is looked upon by one generation as the apex of human knowledge is often considered an absurdity by the next, and that which is regarded as a superstition in one century, may form the basis of science for the following one." *(Theophrastus Paracelsus.)*

PREFACE.

IT is a fact not entirely unknown to those who have studied nature, that there is a certain law of periodicity, according to which forms disappear and the truths which they contained reappear again, embodied in new forms. Seasons go and come, civilizations pass away and grow again, exhibiting the same characteristics possessed by the former, sciences are lost and rediscovered, and the science of medicine forms no exception to this general rule. Many valuable treasures of the past have been buried in forgetfulness; many ideas that shone like luminous stars in the sky of ancient medicine have disappeared during the revolution of thought, and begin to rise again on the mental horizon, where they are christened with new names and stared at in surprise as something supposed never to have existed before.

Ages of spirituality have preceded the past age of materiality, and other eras of higher spiritual thought are certain to follow. During these preceding ages many eminently valuable truths were known, which have been lost sight of in modern times, and although the popular science of the present, which deals with the external appearances of physical nature, is undoubtedly greater than that of former times, a study of the ancient books on medicine shows that the sages of former times knew more of the fundamental laws of nature than what is admitted to-day.

There is a great science and a little science; one that flies around the spires of the temple of wisdom, another that penetrates into the sanctuary; both are right in their places; but the one is superficial and popular, the other profound and mysterious; the one makes a great deal of clamour and show, the other is silent and not publicly known.

There are progressive and there are conservative scientists. There are those whose genius carries them forward and who dare to explore new realms of knowledge; while the conservative class merely collects what has been produced by others. An explorer must be a scientist; but not every scientist is an explorer. The majority of our modern schools of medicine produce nothing new, but merely deal in goods in whose production they had no share. They resemble the shop of a huckster who knows nothing else but the goods which are in his shop. The shelves are filled with popular theories, fashionable beliefs, patented systems, and occasionally we find an old article that went out of fashion, labelled with a new name and advertised as something new, and the proprietor volubly praises his goods, being as proud of them as if he had made them himself, while he ignores or denounces everything that is not to be found in his shop. But the real lover of truth is not contented to live upon the fruits that have grown in the gardens of others; he gathers the materials he finds, not merely for the purpose of enjoying their possession, but for the purpose of using them as steps to ascend nearer to the fountain of eternal truth.

The present work is an attempt to call the attention of those who follow the profession of medicine to this higher aspect of science and to certain forgotten treasures of the past, of which an abundance may be found in the works of Theophrastus Paracelsus. Many of the ideas advanced therein, old as they are, will appear new and strange; for everyone is familiar only with that which is within his own mental horizon and which he is capable of grasping. The subject treated is so grand, unlimited and sublime, as to render it impossible in a limited work of this kind to deal with it in an exhaustive manner; but we hope that what little has been collected in the following pages will be sufficient to indicate the way to the acquisition of that higher mystic science, and to a better understanding of the true constitution of man.

CONTENTS.

V.
THE MEDICINE OF THE FUTURE.

INTRODUCTION.

"There are two kinds of knowledge. There is a medical science and there is a medical wisdom. To the animal man belongs the animal comprehension; but the understanding of divine mysteries belongs to the spirit of God in him." (Theophrastus Paracelsus, *"De Fundamento Sapientiæ."*)

A GREAT deal has been written in modern books on pathology about the difficulty of defining the word *"disease."* The dictionary calls it "lack or absence of ease, pain, uneasiness, distress, trial, trouble," &c., but against either of these definitions objections may be raised. James Paget says: "Ease and disease, well and ill, and all their synonyms are relative terms, of which none can be fixed unconditionally. If there could be fixed a standard of health, all deviations from it might be called diseases; but a chief characteristic of living bodies is not fixity, but variation by self-adjustment to a wide range of varying circumstances, and among such self-adjustments it is not practicable to make a line separating those which may reasonably be called healthy from those which may as reasonably be called disease."

To this occult science answers that *such a standard of health exists for us as soon as we recognise the unity and supremacy of the law; that the results of obedience to the law are harmony and health, and the results of disobedience are called discords or disease.*

Shakespeare says:—

> "The heavens themselves, the planets and this centre
> Observe degree, priority and place,
> Insisture, course, proportion, season, form,
> Office, and custom, in all line of order."
> —*(Troilus and Cressida,* 1. 3.)

If we regard the order, which "is Heaven's first law," as the creation of the self-adjustment of accidentally arising circumstances, leaving out of consideration the fundamental Unity of the All and its one purpose, we would then probably find various laws of order in the universe, being essentially different from each other; and it would be difficult to know which of these laws it would be best to follow; but if we recognise in the order that rules all things a manifestation of one eternal law of order and harmony, the function of Supreme Wisdom acting in nature but not being the product of nature, it will remain for us only to know that supreme Law and obey it. The universe is only one, and is ruled by only one source of all laws; but there are many unities within the constitution of this great Unity; they constitute as many selves within Self, whose separate interests are not identical with that of the whole, and therefore the order obeyed by these temporary selves is not the same as that of the eternal whole. Thus the battle for existence, far from being the cause of the order observable in the world, is in fact the cause of the disorder existing therein.

If man, like his divine prototype, were a perfect unity, a manifestation of will and thought identified and one, there would be only one law to obey: the law of his divine nature; he would he forever in harmony with himself; there would be no disharmonious elements in his nature, seeking to create an order of their own, and thereby causing discords and disease; but man is a compound being, there are many elements in his nature, each representing to a certain extent an independent form of will, and the more one of these modifications of will succeeds in departing from the order that constitutes the whole, and to enact, be it intelligently or instinctively, a will of its own, the greater will be the disharmony which it causes within the whole organism and the greater will be the disease.[1] "A house divided against itself will fall." *Disease is the disharmony which follows the disobedience to the law; the restoration consists in restoring the harmony by a return to obedience to the law of order which governs the whole.*

The key to the cure of diseases is therefore in the understanding of the fundamental law which governs the nature of man, and for this purpose it is necessary that a rational system of medicine should know the constitution of man; not only that of his physical body, which is merely the lower part of the house wherein he dwells; but the whole physical, astral and mental constitution of that being called "Man," which is still the greatest mystery to science, and of which little more than the anatomy, the physiological functions and the chemical composition of the material organs and substances composing his corporeal form is either known to or taught by our modern

---

[1] *Jacob Boehme* says: "If an essence (a form of will-substance) enters into another whose nature is of a different character, an antagonism is created and a strife for supremacy ensues. One quality disrupts the other, which ultimately causes the death of the form; for whatever is not in harmony cannot live eternally; but whatever is in perfect harmony has no elements of destruction within itself; for in such an organism all the elements love each other, and love is the creator and preserver of life."—"Mysterium magnum," xxi. 5.

academies.

Great progress has been made by modern science in investigating all the minor details of the shell which man occupies during his life upon this planet; but as regards the inhabitant of that house, the inner man, who is neither wholly material nor wholly spiritual, the ancient sages knew more about his true nature than is ever dreamed of in our medical schools, and it will be undoubtedly worth while to examine their views. Moreover, if the outward body of man is, as they teach, only the outward expression of the qualities and functions of a more interior and invisible human organism; then it appears that many bodily diseases, such as are not caused by direct physical injuries, are the results of disorders existing within that inner organism, and as every true physician should seek to know the causes of diseases, and not merely destroy their external effects, such a knowledge of the "causal body" of man, whose visible image is his "phenomenal form," may open a new field for pathology and therapeutics, from which a rich harvest may be gathered for the benefit of mankind.

I.
THE CONSTITUTION OF MAN.

FROM times immemorial the sages have taught that we shall never know immortal truth, if we do not discover it within our own selves. Experience has long ago corroborated this theory, for in spite of all progress in scientific researches concerning the nature of Man, and which were carried on by means of researches in the external kingdom of nature, the real constitution of Man and that which constitutes his essential being has not yet been discovered. We know that from the ovum the fœtus, from the fœtus the child, from the child the body of man becomes developed; we know the order in which these processes take place; but we seem to know nothing about the powers that produce them. Such an alchemical trick of nature as to make a man grow out of a cell in which no man is contained would seem absurd, incredible and miraculous, and would be believed by nobody, if it were not a well-known fact, and being of daily occurrence it has ceased to appear surprising, so that it appears now strange if anyone wonders how such a thing is possible.

Horne says: "By a silent, unseen, mysterious process, the fairest flower of the garden springs from a small insignificant seed." A similar mysterious process takes place in the evolution of the human body. All these processes are evidently the effects of the action of a cause adequate to produce them; to deny this would be identical with affirming the self-evident absurdity, that something could grow out of nothing, and the law of logic furthermore makes it clear that although a physical cause can produce a physical effect, a living body can only be produced by a living power, an intellectual organism by an intelligent being. Whether or not the animal body of man has evolved from the lower animal kingdom, or whether certain animals are the products of a perversion and degradation of the nature of man, does not concern us at present. What we know is, that no life and intelligence can become manifest in a form unless these powers are contained therein, and we also know that life cannot be created by death nor can intelligence be created by that which has no intelligence.

But if popular science confessedly knows nothing about the origin of the manifestation of life, nothing about what is vaguely termed "soul," nothing about the nature and origin of the mind (whose functions are required for the purpose of enabling the brain to investigate such things) nothing about the spirit and nothing about the higher constitution of man, whose external expression and symbol is his physical body; it will not be inappropriate to apply to other sources for information and hear what the ancient sages taught concerning the principles that go to make up the constitution of man. *The first requisite of a rational and perfect system of a medicine is a thorough knowledge of the whole constitution of man; of the whole, and not merely of a part of his nature.*

The ancient Indian sages compared man to a lotus flower, whose home is the water (the world), whose roots draw their nutriment from the earth (material nature), while it raises its head to the light (the spiritual kingdom), from which it receives the power to unfold the powers latent in its constitution.

A great deal has already been said in Theosophical literature about the sevenfold constitution of man: but for the sake of completeness we will delineate it again.

1. *Rupa.* The physical body, the vehicle of all the other "principles" during life.

2. *Prana.* Life or vital principle.

3. *Linga Sharira.* The astral body. The ethereal image or counterpart of the physical body, the "phantom body."

4. *Kama rupa.* The animal soul. The seat of animal desires and passions. In this principle is centred the life of the animal and mortal man.

5. *Manas.* Mind. Intelligence. The connecting link between the mortal and immortal man.

6. *Buddhi.* The spiritual soul. The vehicle of pure universal spirit.

7. *Atma.* Spirit.   The radiation of the Absolute. (For further explanation see: H. P. Blavatsky, "Key to Theosophy.")

Goethe says: "A word comes in very conveniently when a conception is absent." In our material age the very meaning of terms signifying spiritual powers and conditions has become lost and perverted; "God" is supposed to mean an unnatural supernatural being outside of Nature; "Faith" has become credulity and belief in the opinions of others; "Hope" has become personal greed; "Love" is supposed to be selfish desire, etc., etc. It is therefore not surprising if the above terms are in-comprehensible to many or misinterpreted by them, for they all represent certain states of consciousness, and no one can know a state of consciousness which he has never experienced. Therein is contained the mystery.

The philosophers of the middle ages symbolised these seven principles by the signs of seven "planets" from which seven cosmic bodies visible in the sky received their names; and if this is understood, it will at once become clear that those who deny the sevenfold division of the planets, only expose their own ignorance and misconceptions. No one can really criticise that which he does not understand; but self-conceit imagines itself to be superior to everything, and thinks itself wiser than all the sages; forgetting that Shakespeare says: *"The fool thinks he is wise, but the wise man knows himself to be a fool." (As You Like It,* V., i.)

The ancients based their science of medicine upon the re-cognition of a universal, eternal, self-existent, self-conscious cause, the source of universal life, where popular modern medicine recognises only the outcome of a blind force. The secret medicine of the ancients was therefore a religious[1] science, while modern popular medicine recognises no religious element and therefore no real truth. To separate science from religious truth is to put it upon an irrational basis; for "religion" means the relation which man bears to his divine origin. To leave out of sight the source from which he originated is to ignore his true nature and to relegate medicine to the realm of the lowest plane of his existence; namely, that of his most gross and material form. This is exactly the position which modern medicine occupies at present, and there is nothing that can elevate it higher than a recognition of the higher nature in man, and a re-discovery of divine truth. Such a higher knowledge was formerly considered necessary for the purpose of constituting a real physician, and for this reason the practice of medicine was in the hands of those who were born physicians, sages and saints by the power of the true grace of God, while among popular practitioners there are, now as then, many dunces and rascals, having neither spirituality nor morality; for what the modern physician of the materialistic school requires for his success is a certain amount of memorizing of the contents of his books, so as to enable him to pass his examination, and a talent to profit by the credulity of the people.

---

[1] Let it be clearly understood that by using the term "religious" we do not refer to any of the existing systems of religious doctrines or forms of worship; but to the spiritual recognition of divine truth.

When the ancients spoke of "seven planets," they referred to seven spiritual but nevertheless substantial states, of which popular science knows nothing but their external, manifestation in the realm of phenomena. It has truly been said that no one ever saw even the *earth;* that which we see is merely a manifestation or appearance of a spiritual principle called "earth" ♁ The real essence of "matter" is beyond the conception of the terrestrial mind.

Seen from this point of view, the "seven planets" in the constitution of man as well as in the constitution of nature as a whole, represent the following elements, powers, essences, or forms of existence:—

I. ♄ *Saturn (Prakriti).* Matter; the substance and material element in all things in all the three kingdoms of nature (the physical, astral and spiritual plane). It is invisible and known only by means of its manifestation. It is that which gives fixity and solidity, it is substantiality itself.

II. ☾ *Luna,* "the Moon" *(Linga).* The "ethereal or astral" body of man; the kingdom of dreams, fancies, illusions, in which exists only the reflection of the true life and light of the sun; it also represents intellectual speculation without wisdom (recognition of truth), and the forms belonging to that kingdom are as changeable as are the opinions of men.

III. ☉ *Sol,* "the Sun" *(Prana).* Life on the physical and spiritual plane *(Jiva).* The centre of the planetary system.[1] It is that which produces the manifestations or activity of life upon every plane of existence.

♂ *Mars (Kama).* The passional, emotional, animal element in man and in nature; the seat of desire and self-will; that which becomes manifest as greed, envy, anger, lust and selfishness in all its forms; but which is also a source of strength. There are many diseases caused by the excessive or irregular action of powers belonging to this kingdom; when by combining with ♄ they become of a terrestrial nature.

☿ *Mercury (Manas).* The Mind; the principle of intelligence manifesting itself as intellectual power in the kingdom of mind;

---

[1] The order here adopted is to facilitate the comparison with the above given classification; the planets not being stationary, but shifting their positions and significations according to the aspects we take.

giving in its combination ♄ with rise to earthly thoughts, but in combination with ♀ constituting spiritual knowledge.

♃ *Jupiter (Buddhi)*. The principle which manifests itself as spiritual power, be it for good or for evil. Reason, intuition, faith, firmness, recognition of truth.

♀ *Venus (Atma)*. The principle which in its purity manifests itself as universal divine love, it being identical with divine self-knowledge. If united with ☿ (intelligence) it constitutes wisdom. Acting within the animal plane it produces animal instincts, and upon the physical plane it causes the attractions of opposite polarities, chemical affinities, &c., &c.

All this is said merely to indicate the key to this kind of science; for the combinations in which these principles may enter, and the modifications of their manifestations under different conditions are almost innumerable; neither can this spiritual science be taught to a mind *(Manas)* unillumined by the light of the higher understanding *(Buddhi)*. The practical study and application of anything requires first of all the possession of the object, and if this is true in regard to physical objects, it is no less true in regard to spiritual principles, whose nature can only be known when their presence is realised within one's own consciousness. The higher aspects of all of these powers belong to the higher nature of man, and he who desires to know and apply these laws in the practice of medicine, must first of all seek to develop his own higher nature by freeing himself from the elements that govern his lower nature; in other words, he must enter from the animal-human into the human-divine state, to which the true physician belongs.

One of such adept-physicians was *Theophrastus Paracelsus,* the great reformer of medicine of the sixteenth century, who is properly regarded as the father of modern medicine, although his successors are still far from realising the truths which he taught, and will, on the whole, perhaps not grow up to an understanding of his doctrines for centuries to come.[1] He was far in advance not only of the science of his days, but also of that of our present

---

[1] Even of his cotemporaneous disciples there were few capable of grasping his ideas and of leading the life necessary for that purpose. He says: "Twenty-one of my servants have become victims of the executioner (the spirit of this world); Gode may help them! Only a few have thus far remained with me." ("Defensio," VI.)

days; for although he may have known less than we do in regard to the phenomenal appearances of the manifestations of life on this planet, he knew a great deal more than our modern science in regard to the causes of these manifestations and in regard to the *inner* nature of things. He was and still is ridiculed and belittled by those who were and are not capable of understanding him; but he proved the truth of his theories by performing cures which even modern medicine with all its new acquisitions cannot perform.[1] He was the first to abolish a system of unmitigated quackery, based upon mere empiricism, the remnants of which exist even to-day. He was hated and persecuted by the quacks and pretenders of those times, who did a lucrative business, thriving upon the ignorance of the public, as some are doing to-day, and the vilifications and calumnies thrown out against him by such still inspire the opinions of many in regard to his person, although we may safely believe that few of his critics have ever read his books and still fewer have understood them. Numerous biographies have been written about him and his personal habits, and it seems that the majority of his critics have been able to comprehend that when he died he left a pair of leather pantaloons to his heirs; but as to his philosophy, this is a *terra incognita,* which surpasses their understanding; neither could such a knowledge of the secret sciences be expected from anybody knowing nothing about the fundamental principles in the constitution of man.

Whether Paracelsus obtained his knowledge in the East, as has been claimed, or whether it was revealed to him by his own perception of truth, does not concern us; but there can be no doubt that he knew that sevenfold classification, for we find him speaking of the following seven aspects of man:—

1. *The Corpus,* or the elementary body of man. *(Limbos.)*

2. *The Mumia,* or the ethereal body; the vehicle of life. *(Evestrum.)*

3. *The Archæus.* The essence of life. *Spiritus Mundi* in Nature and *Spiritus Vitae* in man.

4. *The Sidereal body;* made up of the influences of the "stars."

5. *Adech.* The inner man or the thought-body, made of the flesh of Adam.

6. *Aluech.* The spiritual body, made of the flesh of Christ;

---

[1] See "The Life of Theophrastus Paracelsus," London, 1887.

also called "the man of the new Olympus."

7. *Spiritus.* The universal Spirit.

There is hardly a page in the philosophical writings of Paracelsus which does not refer to the twofold nature of man, his terrestrial and celestial aspect, and of the necessity of the development of his higher nature and superior (spiritual) understanding.

"Above all, we must pay attention to the fact that there are two kinds of spirit in man. (One originating in nature, the other coming from heaven.) Man ought to be a human being according to the spirit of (divine) life and not according to the (terrestrial) spirit of the *Limbus.* It is a truth that (the heavenly) man is an image of God, having in him a divine spirit (life). In all other respects he is an animal, having as such an animal spirit. These two are opposed to each other, but one of the two is bound to succumb. Man is destined to be a human being and not an animal, and if he is to be a human being, he must live within the spirit of (immortal) life and do away with the animal spirit." ("Philosophia Occulta," Lib. I., Prologue.)

The mysteries of the inner temple of nature are not accessible to the vulgar and the profane, because every being can realise only that which corresponds to its own nature. To penetrate into the realm of truth a true soul is required; an animal can realise only the animal side of existence.

One well known medical authority on a recent occasion said:

"Paracelsus, who pronounced the anatomy of the dead body to be useless,"[1] and sought for the basis of life *(immortality)* as the highest goal of knowledge, demanded contemplation *(spiritual)* before all else, and just as he himself arrived in this way at the metaphysical construction of the *Archaeus,* so he unchained among his followers a wild and absolutely fruitless mysticism."[2]

For this unchaining of mysticism, not Paracelsus is to blame,

---

[1] This is not correct; Paracelsus says: "The anatomy of man is twofold. One aspect consists in dissecting the body, so as to find out the position of its bones, muscles, veins, &c.; but this is the least important; the other is more important, and means to introduce a new life into the human organism; to see the transmutations taking place therein, to know what the blood is and what kind of ⊖, ♄ and ☿ (Salt, Sulphur and Mercury) it contains." ("Paramirum," Lib. I. Cap. 6.)

[2] Prof. Rud. Virchow's lecture on Pathology, delivered in London, March 6th, 1893

but the incapacity of his followers, whose animal minds were not capable of becoming illumined by the spirit of truth. Whenever the terrestrial mind seeks to grasp the spirit of wisdom, and being unable to rise to the perception of divine truth to drag it down to its own level, a wild and absolutely fruitless and foolish mysticism will be the result. With the same right we may say that the doctrines of Christ filled the world with superstition, causing the crimes of the crusades, the horrors of the inquisition, and sectarian intolerance. It is not the fault of the truth if it is misunderstood.

The vast majority of mankind seek for knowledge for the purpose of deriving from its possession some personal benefit; be it the acquisition of wealth or luxury, the gratification of ambition, the desire to parade before the world as a being in possession of something great, or for the purpose of satisfying a laudable scientific curiosity. But the acquisition of medical wisdom requires a love of the truth, and love means self-sacrifice. The acquisition of wisdom is therefore possible only if the illusive self with all its desires is sacrificed to it. The way to wisdom can be shown; but wisdom can only be taught by wisdom itself; he who loves the realm of illusions cannot see its true light. How many of the would-be followers of Jesus of Nazareth have become Christs, and who can understand the profundity of his thoughts and exercise his divine powers, but he who has become like him? None of the would-he followers of Paracelsus have grown to he like this master, none of the representatives of modern medical science have penetrated deeply into his wisdom.

Popular medical science, being based upon the objective observation of phenomena, knows more about the realm of visible nature (Maya) than was known at the time of Paracelsus; but the reason why this popular medical science, in spite of the aids which it received from chemistry and physiology, is still incapable of performing the cures which were performed by Paracelsus, is because its followers only speculate and draw inferences, while they do not cultivate that spiritual power of soul knowledge which is called "interior contemplation,"[1] but

---

[1] The word "contemplation"—from *con*=with, and *templum*=temple—means evidently not mere objective observation, but an indwelling in the same temple with the truth which is to be known, an identification of subject and object in the light of divine wisdom, the temple of truth. The attainment of knowledge by such

which Paracelsus called the *Faith;* a faculty which is at present so entirely unknown that even an explanation of the meaning of this term is exceedingly difficult. It is a power which belongs neither to the physical, nor to the animal, nor to the intellectual nature in man, but to the spiritual man (Atma-Buddhi-Manas); to that higher part of his being, which in the vast majority of mankind, however intellectual they may be, has not yet awakened into life, but is still latent, buried in the tomb of materiality into which the light of divine truth cannot penetrate.

"What are ye men in your own powers but nothing? If you wish to obtain strength take it from faith. If you have faith as big as a mustard seed, you will be as strong as the spirits, and although you now appear as men, your faith will make your strength and power equal to the spirits such as were also in Samson. For by means of our faith we become spirits ourselves, and whatever we accomplish that surpasses our (terrestrial) nature is done by the power of faith acting through us as a spirit and transforming us into spirits." ("De Origin, Morb. Invisib." Introduction.)

Man, even if he obtains occasionally a glimpse of divine truth, is only too prone to forget it again at the next moment, as the action of his terrestrial mind is stronger in him than that of his spirit, and it seems therefore necessary to be reminded over and over again that the faith of which Paracelsus speaks is not the illusory faith of the brain, the product of speculation, but a power belonging to those few living spirits walking within this sleeping world. As physical powers belong to the physical and terrestrial man, so spiritual powers belong to the spiritual man who must be born before he can know and exercise these powers. As yet there appear to be few even among our eminent scientists and successful practitioners who have become regenerated in the spirit of truth and filled with the light of divine wisdom, and if there are any such, we would ask all the students of medicine to follow their example and by learning the great art of self-control to become masters over their own nature and over the nature of others. Humanity is only one, and the

---

a contemplation is only possible for those whose spiritual perception is open. A blind person may dwell forever in the temple of truth without being able to know it. To those who by an unfoldment of their spirituality have attained this power of contemplation, its sufficiency for the attainment of spiritual knowledge is self-evident and requires no arguments. Those who do not possess this power will find it difficult to understand the meaning of this term, and suppose it to be imagination.

realization of this truth will open a new field for the science of medicine in the future. That part of us which lives within the heart of others is our own truest and "most profound Self."[1] If this self, which lives in the hearts of others, has awakened to its own consciousness, it will realize its own universal existence and its own power to act within those in whom it lives. Thus the physician, having become self-conscious of his own higher nature, will become a saviour for all the rest of mankind, not only in regard to their moral evils, but also in regard to their physical ills; for the spirit and soul and body of man do not live separately; they are one organic whole, as is the body of humanity, even though the personalities constituting that body are separated from each other by the illusion of form.

---

[1] Herder.

II.

THE FOUR PILLARS OF MEDICINE.

THE pillars upon which the practice of modern medicine rests, are

1. *A knowledge of the physical body of man,* the arrangements of its organs (anatomy), their physiological functions (physiology) and the visible changes which take place in them when a disease becomes manifest (pathology).

2. *A certain amount of acquaintance with physical science,* chemistry, botany, mineralogy, etc., in fact with all that embodies a knowledge of the outward relations which the things in this phenomenal world bear to each other and to the body of man, (therapeutics).

3. A certain amount of acquaintance with *the views and opinions of modern accepted medical authorities,* however erroneous they may be.

4. A certain amount of *judgment and aptitude* to put the acquired theories into practice.

All this is very well as far as it goes; but it may be seen at once that all the knowledge required of a modern practitioner refers only to the external plane of existence; the animal body of man and its physical surroundings. As to a science of "psychology," to call that which goes by that name as such at present, is a misnomer; for there can be no science of the soul as long as the existence of a soul *(pysche)* is not recognized.[1] The invisible, spiritual or causal body within the nature of man is entirely ignored by science, and even if any modern physician personally believes in a soul, he will almost without exception consider this subject as belonging exclusively to the Church, and as something with which science has nothing to do.

Nevertheless, if the term "religion" means the knowledge of the relation which the outward terrestrial man bears to the

---

[1] Only very recently in the courts of Vienna during a sensational trial in regard to the state of *non compos mentis,* concerning a nobleman, who left a considerable fortune to his servants, the total ignorance of the experts on "psychology" regarding all matters concerning the soul, and their total incapacity to judge of the character and motives of a person, became so plain and was exposed in such a ludicrous manner, that it became the public opinion, which was also expressed by the judge, that the custom of calling in medical men as experts in such things ought to be abandoned, and that actors, novel-writers, or such as possess more capacity to know the motives of human nature should be selected for that purpose.

creative power in him, his own inner Self, which is the seat of not only his spiritual but also the indirect source of his physical life; it would seem that a knowledge of that religion which teaches the nature of this true inner and immortal being, and also the links which connect that higher nature with the physical form, would be an indispensable and most important part of a true science and system of medicine based upon the recognition of truth; and although theory precedes practice, this knowledge should not be merely of that theoretical kind which is only imaginary and not real, and which in persons who are attempting to grasp things which they are not able to realise produces a wild and absolutely fruitless mysticism; but it should be of that kind which through experience constitutes self-knowledge, and which is possible only through the realization of the possession of the ideals one wishes to know.

According to Theophrastus Paracelsus the following are the four pillars of medicine:—

I.—PHILOSOPHIA.

The term "Philosophy" comes from *phileo,* to love, and *sophia,* wisdom, and its true meaning is the love of wisdom and the knowledge resulting there from; for love itself is knowledge; it is the recognition of self in another form; the love of wisdom is the recognition by wisdom in man of the same principle of wisdom that is manifested in Nature, and from this recognition springs the realisation of the knowledge of truth. True philosophy is therefore not that thing which at present goes by that name, which consists in wild speculations about the mysteries of Nature for the purpose of gratifying scientific curiosity; a system in which there is a great deal of self-love but very little love of the truth, and whose followers, by means of logic and argument, inferences, theories, postulates, hypotheses, inductions and deductions seek, so to say, to break through the back windows in the temple of truth, or to peep through the keyhole for the purpose of seeing the goddess unveiled. This speculative philosophy does not constitute real knowledge. It constitutes that artificial building of philosophy and so-called science, founded upon arguments and opinions, which change their aspect in every century, and of which Paracelsus said that "the things which are looked upon by one generation as the apex of human knowledge are found to be an absurdity by the next, and that which is regarded as a superstition in one century forms the basis of science of the following one." All information gained by means whose basis is not a love of truth does not constitute immortal knowledge or true theosophy; but serves only for temporal purposes and as ornaments for egotism, springing as it does from the love of the illusion of self and having illusions for its object.

The whole of nature is a manifestation of truth; but it requires the eye of wisdom to see the truth and not merely its delusive appearance. The philosophy of which Paracelsus speaks consists in the power of recognizing the truth in all things independent of any books or authorities, all of which can only serve to show us the way to avoid errors and how to remove the obstacles in our path; but which cannot make us realise that which we do not realise in ourselves. He who is not labouring under a load of misconceptions and erroneous teachings, requires no other book than the book of nature to teach him the truth. There are few who can read the book of nature in the light of nature; because having had their minds filled with perverted images and false views, they have themselves become unnatural, and the light of nature cannot penetrate into their souls; living in the false light of the moonshine of speculation and sophistry, they have lost their receptivity for the light of the truth. Such philosophers live in illusions and dreams but do not know that which is real:

"There is upon this earth nothing more noble and more capable of giving perfect happiness than a true knowledge of nature and its foundation. Such a knowledge produces a valuable physician, but it should be a part of his constitution and not an artificial fabric attached to him like a coat; he must himself be born out of the fountain of that philosophy which cannot be acquired by artificial means." (See "De Generatione hominum," I. Preface.)

A knowledge based upon the opinion or experience of another is merely a belief, but does not constitute real knowledge. Books and lectures may serve to give us advice, but they cannot endow us with the power of knowing the truth; they may serve us as useful guides, but a belief in the statements of others should not be mistaken for self-knowledge, such as arises only from the self-recognition of truth, and which by means of a love of the truth ought to be cultivated above all else.

To this realm of Philosophy belong all the natural sciences referring to external phenomena, in the knowledge of which a great deal of progress seems to have been made since the time of Paracelsus. To this phenomenal science belongs the anatomy, physiology, the chemistry of the physical body and all that concerns the interrelations of the phenomena existing in the grand phantasmagoria of living and corporeal images called the sensual world. But behind this sensual world there is a more interior super-sensual world, ignored by popular science, of which the former is the external expression; the processes taking place in this interior light of nature, mirror themselves in the light of the external world, and those souls whose inner perceptions have become developed in consequence of an awakening of the "inner man," do not require the observation of external phenomena for the purpose of drawing inferences in regard to their internal causes, because they know the interior causes and processes and also the external appearances which they will produce. Thus there is an external and an internal medical science, a science concerning the astral and a science concerning the physical body of man. The former occupies itself with the patient, the latter, so to say, with the clothes which he wears.

To render this still more plain, let us illustrate it by an example. Let us imagine a magic lantern capable of projecting living and corporeal images upon a living screen. External science occupies itself only with these images, the relations which they bear to each other and the changes taking place between them; but it knows nothing about the slides in the lantern upon which are the types of these visible images, and it entirely ignores the light which causes their projection upon that screen; but he who sees the slides with its pictures and knows the source of the light which produces these shadow pictures does not need to study the shadows for the purposes of drawing inferences and speculating in regard to their causes. Thus there is a superficial science which is at present the object of pride of the world, and a secret science of which next to nothing is publicly known, but which is known to the wise and revealed by one's own perception of truth.[1]

---

[1] We may read at any time that the views of the ancients in regard to this or that were "very vague"; while in fact the vagueness is with the critic who does not understand what the views of the ancients were. Words are made for the purpose of expressing ideas, and if the ideas are not perceived the words are only misleading. If we interpret the meaning of a term according to our own fancy, we shall find therein only the misconception put into it by ourselves, but not the

Truths must be perceived before they can be intellectually grasped, and therefore this greater and higher science cannot be learned in books, nor be taught in lectures at college, it is the result of a development of man's higher perception, belonging to his higher nature, and characterises the born physician. Without this superior faculty, known in its initial stage as the power of "intuition," a medical practitioner can find occupation only in the outer yard of the temple, picking up useful grains among the rubbish; but he cannot enter the temple in which nature herself teaches her divine mysteries. The minute details of this rubbish have been studied by modern popular science, whose attention has been so much absorbed thereby that the temple of truth itself has been forgotten and the nature of Life has become a mystery to those who only study its external manifestations.

It will hardly be necessary to say that the above is not intended to discourage the study of phenomena; for those who have not the power of reaching higher will gain nothing by remaining ignorant of external appearances; but it is intended to show that a science referring merely to the phenomena of terrestrial life and ultimate results is not the summit of all possible knowledge; for beyond the realm of visible phenomena there is a far more extensive realm open to all who are capable of entering: the realm of truth, of which only the inverted images are seen in the kingdom of external phenomena.

The natural science of the ancient mystics, owing to their deeper penetration into the so-called supersensual realm, was not limited to the world which we see with our bodily eyes; for they recognised four worlds or planes of existence within each other, each of them having its own forms of life and inhabitants, namely:—

(*a.*) *The physical visible world,* being only the reflection of the three higher ones.

(*b.*) *The astral world,* or the psychic realm.

(*c.*) *The world of mind,* or the spiritual realm.

(*d.*) *The divine state,* the kingdom of God, or the celestial world.

As we perceive the existence of a mineral, vegetable and animal kingdom upon the sensual plane,[1] so they, by the faculty

---

original meaning.

[1] We call this the *sensual plane,* merely because it includes that which is perceived by the senses of our *physical* body. If the senses of the *astral* form are

of the developed inner sight perceived and described within this world four kingdoms, or four spiritual, and to us invisible, states of existence, which in their outward manifestation are called: *Earth, Water, Fire, Air.*

"We will show you that we are not the only intelligent beings possessing the world, but that our possessions extend over only one-fourth of it. Not that this world were three times greater than we know it to be; but there are in it still three-fourth parts which we do not occupy, and their inhabitants are not inferior to us in intelligence; the only thing of which we may be proud, is that Christ (the light of divine wisdom) has taken his habitation in us and clothed himself in our form, as he might have chosen another nation (another class of Elementals) for that purpose." *(Paracelsus, "Of* the generation of conscious beings in the universal mind," I. Preface.)

All this, however, does not strictly belong to the present purpose of this work, and is merely mentioned so as to make room for the conception that nature is far greater than the limits assigned to it by material science, and that, as a certain philosopher said: "that which is known is only like a grain of sand on the shore of the ocean of the unknown."

II. ASTRONOMIA.

"Astronomy" means the knowledge of the stars, and to the conception of the modern mind it is the science of "celestial bodies," such as are seen at night on the sky; but to the ancient philosophers all visible things were the symbols and representations of invisible powers, thoughts and ideas, and the expression "Astronomy," as used by Paracelsus, is, therefore, something quite different from the science of the star-gazers, and refers to the various states of the mind existing in the macrocosm of nature as well as in the microcosm of man. "The very word "celestial" or "heavenly," refers to something superior to our grossly material nature, and an idea of what are the "stars" with which ancient astronomy and astrology deal, may be formed by studying the signification of the planets referred to in the previous chapter on the Constitution of Man.

The Astronomy of Paracelsus, therefore, does not deal with

---

developed, the *astral plane* will also be our *sensual* plane. There can be no knowledge without perception, and no perception without a sense for that purpose. A system of philosophy based merely upon speculation, and without any perception of truth, is no philosophy at all; but consist merely of vagaries, illusions and dreams.

corporeal, material, visible, cosmic bodies; but with *vivtutes* (virtues) or powers and *semina* (germs), or essences, all of which are spiritual and substantial; because a power without substance is inconceivable; "power and substance," "matter and force" being convertible terms, states of one unity, divided only in our conception of the modes of its manifestation. A "star", in fact, means a *state,* and a "fixed star" a fixed state of a power in nature; or as it is called in Sanscrit, a *Tattwa,* which means a state of *That* or Being, and as all Being is a manifestation of Life or Consciousness, the "stars" are certain states of that universal Life or All-consciousness, in other words, states of the *Mind.*

"You should know that the constellations of the planets and stars on the sky, with all the firmament, do not cause the growth of our body, our colour, appearance, or behaviour; and have nothing to do with our virtues and qualities. Such an idea is ridiculous; the motion of Saturn interferes with nobody's life, and makes it neither longer nor shorter, and, even if there had never been a planet called "Saturn" on the sky, there would be people born having saturnine natures. For all that the planet Mars is of a fiery nature, Nero was not its child, and although they are of the same nature (the same kind of energy being manifested in either of them) neither one of them received it from the other." ("De Ente Astrorum," *Paramirum* C. I. 2.)

Perhaps it will not be out of place, for the purpose of facilitating a comprehension of what Paracelsus meant by the term "Astronomy," to take a glance at the Indian teaching in regard to the *Tattwas.*

According to these doctrines, the Universe is a manifestation of *That* (existence or being), manifesting itself as Life *(Prana)* within the universal *Akâsa* (primordial matter, which, for all practical purposes, may be regarded as the "cosmic ether" of space). Prana manifests itself upon the various planes of existence in various *Tattwas* or forms of existence, corresponding to the principles in the constitution of man enumerated above. Of these seven Tattwas five are manifested, corresponding to the five senses of the human body, and they are called as follows:—[1]

1. *Akasa Tattwa;* the *one* element forming the substantial basis of the other four, and corresponding to that which upon the physical plane becomes ultimately manifested as audible sound.

2. *Vayou Tattwa;* representing the principle which renders

[1] See Rama Prasad's "Nature's Finer Forces."

possible the sensation of feeling or "touch," upon all planes of existence.

3. *Taijas Tattwa;* that form of existence which represents that state which manifests itself upon all planes as Light.

4. *Apas Tattwa;* that principle which renders possible the sensation of taste upon all planes of existence.

Prithivi Tattwa; that principle which renders possible the sensation of smell upon all planes of existence.

Words are altogether insufficient to give an idea on which to form a conception of things which are beyond our intellectual comprehension as long as they do not live in our own consciousness; but we may look upon the seven *Tattwas* as represented by seven modes of vibrations of a cosmic ether, differing from each other not only quantitatively, but qualitatively, so that, for instance, *Akasa Tattwa* has a circular, *Vayou Tattwa* a spiral movement, etc.; but such a conception is quite inadequate, as we have to do with living forces, with states of the universal life or consciousness, manifesting themselves not only as the causes of the five modes of perception on the physical plane, but also upon the higher planes; enabling man, for instance, not only to feel the touch of an object upon the physical plane, but to feel with his astral sense the presence of an object upon the astral plane, and in his heart the touch of a spiritual power; to see not only physical light with the eyes of his body, but things in the astral light with his astral organs of seeing; to see intellectual truths and ideas with the eye of his intellect in the light of his intellect, and spiritual things with the eye of the spirit. In fact, everything that exists is a manifestation of *Tattwas,* or "vibrations of ether;" stationary in its aspect as "matter," progressive in its aspect as "force;" matter is latent energy, force is active substance;[1] everything is life, consciousness, intelligence, dormant or active according to the conditions existing upon the plane upon which it becomes manifest; every substance is mind, and the forms which we see are only the symbols of the thoughts represented therein.

It is not our purpose within the narrow limits of this work to enter into a deeper investigation of this most interesting, sublime, and elevating science, which has been discussed at length in H. P. Blavatsky's "Secret Doctrine"; we merely touch

---

[1] See "Magic, white and black," 4th edition, London, 1893 (Kegan, Paul and Co.).

upon these points for the purpose of calling attention to it, as it represents an aspect and conception of nature immeasurably higher than the one represented by popular science, and therefore attainable only to those whose aspirations reach beyond this grossly material plane.

The "Secret Doctrine" informs us that in the course of evolution, this our planet has only attained its *Kâma-rupa* or animal form of existence, and that the next higher state of *Manas* (mind) has hardly begun to become developed. This may be the reason why the science of mind is at present in its infancy, and grasped only by those gifted spirits who, like Paracelsus and others of his kind, by nobility of character and spirituality have outstripped the rest of mankind in higher knowledge; forming, so to say, the vanguard of the army, as it proceeds into the regions of the—not absolutely unknowable—but the *unknown.*

Modern astronomy teaches the science of the bodies of the planets and stars; the Astronomy of Paracelsus speaks of the spiritual forces represented by those planets, the counterparts of which exist in the constitution of man and as every force in nature acts upon its corresponding element in the nature of man, these universal forces produce certain effects upon those elements in man which exist upon the corresponding plane. Thus for instance it requires no argument to prove that the sun is the source of heat and light and life upon this planet, and that the physical body of man as well as that of the earth receives these energies from the radiations coming from the physical body of the sun; this being the corporeal visible centre of a power existing universally, and whose sphere of activity reaches as far as the limits of our solar system. We all live and have our being physically within the sphere of activity and consequently within the physical elements of the sun; in a similar sense we live and have our being spiritually in the spiritual body and substance of Love, and as the sun of the physical world shines upon our body; so the light of divine wisdom is all around us and ready to penetrate into our soul. Thus Paracelsus teaches that the moon corresponds to the astral body of man, and has certain effects upon it, causing certain states which may ultimately become outwardly manifested as certain moral or physical diseases, and similar correspondencies might be shown to exist between the universal powers represented by the visible planets and the corresponding elements existing in the constitution of man; but however important and interesting this subject may be it finds very little attention on the part of popular medical science, which is far too busy in investigating outward effects of a phenomenal character to find time for attending to that which produces all such phenomena and appearances.[1]

If the Astronomy of Paracelsus were understood, it would be found that man, far from creating his own thoughts, merely remodels the ideas that flow into his mind; that "Thought-transference," far from being a strange and rare occurrence, is as common as the transference of heat; that owing to the oneness of humanity we all feel and think within each other and act out each other's thoughts. We would know better the real causes of crimes, insanity and disease, and find them to be controvertible terms. We might then perhaps also modify our views regarding the supposed free will and the amount of responsibility of man, and know that the power of will is not a myth, and witchcraft and sorcery no more impossible than the magic action of true love.

III.—ALCHEMY.

Not being masters of Alchemy, we are not capable of teaching the science of this pillar of medicine; neither could any information in regard to the way in which certain mysterious powers are used be of any service to those who, not having developed these powers, are not in possession of them. The following remarks are therefore rather intended to show what Alchemy is *not,* than to show what it is; for like every term symbolising a spiritual truth, which ever fell into the hands of the vulgar, so this term has been "besmirched with mud and prostituted openly in the market place,"[2] so as to be now almost beyond recognition.

The ancient alchemists used a mysterious language when speaking about mysterious things, nor could any modern alchemist express in plain language things for which our language has no words and common minds no conception. Children often speak more wisely than they know, sages know

---

[1] The more the minds of men become complicated by attending to a multiplicity of details, the more will they lose sight of simple facts. Thus the action of the sunlight and its various colours, of which each has its special therapeutic qualities, is far too simple a thing to find popular favour.

[2] "The Secret Symbols of the Rosicrucians," II., pp. 16. (Occult Publishing Co., Boston, Mass., 1888).

what they speak, but the half learned speak without knowing. The child receiving gifts from its parents on Christmas eve believes that the Christ has sent these presents, but the grown-up and clever boy becomes sceptical and laughs at that story. In that opinion he may now continue all his life, or he may become still more clever and find that the Christ is divine love, from which the love of his parents originated, inducing them to bestow gifts, and that the story which he believed when a child, was true after all. In the same sense Alchemy is either a truth or a superstition; it merely depends on the definition we give to this term.

Professor Justus von Liebig says: "Alchemy was never anything different from Chemistry," and to this we agree in so far as both deal with substantial things, having certain affinities, and not with anything existing outside of nature; but while ordinary (physical) chemistry employs merely physical (mech-anical) forces for the purpose of composing and decomposing material substances without causing anything new to grow, Alchemy employs the power of life and uses animated forces, establishing conditions under which something visible may grow from something invisible, in the same sense as a tree grows from a seed in the alchemical laboratory of nature. Chemistry and Alchemy are therefore two aspects of one and the same science, the one is the lower, the other the higher part. The chemist who decomposes salt into NA and CL, and recombines it into NA CL, practises chemistry; the gardener establishing in his hot house the conditions under which the seed of a plant of a lower type is made to develop into a plant of a higher type, and the schoolmaster who makes an intelligent being out of a dunce, are practicing Alchemy, because they produce something more noble than the materials employed, out of the latent potencies contained therein.

Without the alchemy of nature no "physiological chemistry " could take place; without the action of a universally existing life principle, no human form could grow out of an ovum or foetus, no child develop into a man. The human stomach is an alchemical laboratory in which miracles are performed which no modern chemist can imitate by merely chemical means; milk and bread are transformed into blood and flesh within the living retort of the human body, and wonders performed which modern chemistry in spite of its progress cannot accomplish, because it does not control the organising power of life.

All that popular belief knows of ancient Alchemy is from the misunderstood writings of the ancients, who purposely wrote in a manner incomprehensible to the uninitiated, or from the writings of pretenders and frauds—for at that time there were as many selfish and ignorant people as there are to-day, wasting their time in useless efforts to apply a spiritual science to material purposes, and seeking to employ powers which they did not possess, in the hope of satisfying their curiosity and their greed. Of this kind of "Alchemy," Paracelsus speaks with the greatest contempt."[1]

For the purpose of practising chemistry physical powers and scientific acquisitions are required; for the purpose of practising alchemy living spiritual powers and wisdom are necessary. Chemistry belongs to the terrestrial man, *the higher aspect of Alchemy belongs to the spiritually regenerated man having passed through the* MYSTIC DEATH *into the resurrection of the true and immortal life.*[2]

As there are three kingdoms in nature, intimately connected with each other, the kingdom of physical nature, the kingdom of the soul of the world (the astral plane), and the kingdom of the self-conscious spirit; so there are three aspects of Alchemy, intimately connected with each other, one belonging to the physical, the other to the astral, and the highest to the spiritual aspect of man. H. P. Blavatsky Says:

"Everything which exists in the world around us is made up of three principles (substances) and four aspects. (The triple synthesis of the seven principles.) As Man is a complex unity, consisting of a body, a rational soul and an immortal spirit, so each object in nature possesses an objective exterior, a vital soul, and a divine spark which is purely spiritual and subjective. Thus, as with all natural objects, so every science has its three fundamental principles and may be applied through all three or by the use of one of them."[3]

These three states of existence in the universe were called by the

---

[1] "Paracelsus," p. 168. (London, 1887: Trubner & Co.

[2] The regenerated spiritual man is not a dream or an unrealisable ideal, but far more substantial than the terrestrial man. *William Law* says: "Where Christ is born or His Spirit rises up in the soul, there all self is denied and obliged to turn out, there all carnal wisdom, arts of advancement, with every pride and glory of this life, are so many heathen idols, all willingly renounced, and the man is not only content, but rejoices to say that his kingdom is not of this world." ("William Law," London, 1893.) See also "Jacob Boehme," page 263. London, 1891.

[3] "Theosophical Siftings." Alchemy. (London: Theo. Pub. Soc., 1891.)

ancient alchemists the *Three Substances,* and symbolized as *Salt, Sulphur,* and *Mercury.*

With the same right as the modern chemist symbolizes his chemical substances by means of letters; such as *O* for oxygen, *H* for hydrogen, *N* for nitrogen, *C* for carbogen,[1] etc., which symbols are incomprehensible to those who do not know what they mean; the ancient alchemists expressed the nature of spiritual essences, powers and principles with which they dealt by certain alchemical signs, such as ⊖ for *Salt,* or the substantial principle in all things, ♁ for *Sulphur,* or the energies contained therein, and ☿ for *Mercury,* or the principle of intelligence latent in everything, whether manifested or not; but the living essences or states in the universe which become manifested upon these three planes they symbolized by the signs of the planets, as has already been specified above. These principles are eternal; but their manifestations differ according to the plane upon which they become manifest. Thus, for instance, love is eternal, manifesting itself in the kingdom of God as divine self-consciousness; upon the astral plane as affection, desire and passion; upon the physical plane as gravitation, attraction, chemical affinity, etc. The power is always the same; but its action appears different under different conditions.

"Above all a physician should know that man exists in three substances. That of which he is made has three aspects. Those three make up the whole man, and they are the man himself and he is they, and out of these three substances he receives all his good and evil concerning his physical body. Thus each thing exists in these three substances, and the three together constitute a body, and there is nothing added to it but the life. If you can see these true substances, you then have the eye by means of which a physician ought to be able to see. To see the exterior only is in the power of everybody; but to see within the interior and discover what is hidden, is an art that belongs to the physician." ("Paramirum," *Lib. I.* s.b.)

Those who have thus far followed our line of reasoning will now be ready to acknowledge that an understanding of this superior science, the acquisition of whose knowledge requires a life-time spent by a superior mind, and whose practice involves the evolution of superior faculties, is not to be obtained by a few

---

[1] We purposely say "carbogen" and not "carbon," because we refer to that invisible element, whose product upon the visible plane is carbon or coal.

hours' perusal of a book on Alchemy, and that only those who are practical alchemists are entitled to judge it. Alchemy, far from being an "exploded humbug," is in fact the noblest object for which all humanity and civilization strives. It is the realization of the highest ideal, a feat which cannot be accomplished by anything less than that ideal itself. H. P. Blavatsky says:—

"When there appeared on earth men endowed with a superior intelligence, they allowed this supreme power (the divine spark) to have full and uncontrolled action, and from it they learnt their first lessons. All that they had to do was to imitate it. But in order to reproduce the same effects by an effort of individual will, they were obliged to develop in their human constitution a (creative) power called KRIYASAKTI *in occult phraseology."*

We should be extremely happy to make the acquaintance of a modern man of science who obeys divine law to such an extent as to let the power of God (the Holy Ghost) have full control over his thoughts, will, and desires. Such a person without selfish desires, without ambition or vanity, without any greed for money or fame, acting as an instrument of divine love, would be a rare specimen of humanity; but unfortunately such a saint and sage will hardly be found in our present generation; for a thousand links tie the human animal to the region of his desires, and how could he who is bound by a thousand chains to the *Moon* employ the energy of the *Sun,* whose influence he will not permit to enter his nature, and which therefore cannot nourish his body and grow into a power in him. Gold and silver may form an alloy; but they never become identical with each other. Thus their spiritual representatives, Divine Wisdom and the carnal intellect, will never be one and the same, although the light of wisdom will throw its reflection upon the terrestrial mind.

As stated before, there are three aspects of *Alchemy:*—

Terrestrial Alchemy. This in its lower aspect includes the whole science of chemistry with all the discoveries that may be made in the future. This alchemy still recognizes four *elements[1],* and the fifth, the one element, from which the four take their

---

[1] As we are not writing for children, it is unnecessary to refute the puerile objection and say that the sixty-four so-called single bodies of chemistry are not elements of nature, although they may be regarded as the elements of the science of chemistry.

origin;[1] in other words four states of matter and a fifth one (partly recognised by science); namely, the solid (substantial), liquid, fluidic, and ethereal state. These are described as follows:—

   a. ▽ *(Earth.)* That which gives substantiality to all things, whether solid, liquid, gaseous, ethereal or spiritual. *(Solidity* or *Stability.)*

   b. ▽ *(Water.)* That state which moves and renders things liquid on either plane of existence. *(Motion).*

   c. △ *(Air.)* That which enables things to assume a gaseous form. *(Extension.)*

   d. △ *(Fire.)* That which endows them with force. *(Energy.)*

   e. ○ *(Ether.)* This fifth element, in which the attributes of all the other states have their basis, will be the principal object for scientific research in the coming centuries, and is in fact the first and the *one* element. These elements represent themselves as the *Tattwas* enumerated in the preceding chapter, and correspond to them as follows, if we adopt the above line of order:—

a. Prithivi.	Solidity. (Earth.)	
b. Apas.	Movement. Bulk. (Water.)	
c. Vayu.	Extension. (Air.)	
d. Taijas.	Energy. Intensity. (Fire.)	
e. Akâsa.	The one *Tattwa* forming the basis of the rest. (Sound)[2]	

---

[1] In everything are there five elements or qualities contained, because everything consists of vibrations of the one element, called by the Alchemists *prima materia*, in which these qualities are latent (potentially contained). Everything is a manifestation of substance. That which is essential in it, is the substance and not the form. Thus for instance that which is essential in a diamond is the carbon but carbon is not composed of diamonds. Carbon is a substance universally distributed in nature in solid, watery, gaseous, fiery form, and all these forms of carbon are certain states of the one element "Carbogen" which in at the root of their existence.

[2] *Vach.*—If we remember that according to the Bible all things were made of the *Word,* and that "the Word was God" (John i., I), we may obtain the key to the understanding of what generated the *Akâsa.*

The limitation of space in these pages, no less than the insufficiency of our experience in regard to this subject, forbids us to enter into a closer investigation of the relations existing between this aspect of Alchemy and physical chemistry; but we have reason to affirm, that we are on the eve of great discoveries, which will to a certain extent revolutionize the popular chemistry of the present day.

Celestial Alchemy.—Even if it were within our power to describe the secrets of celestial alchemy, by means of which the universe was created and which includes the regeneration of man and the attainment of conscious immortality, and if this could be done publicly without profaning those mysteries, the explanation would probably be comprehensible only to those who, knowing it already, do not require it. Those who wish to investigate this subject for the love of wisdom will find the whole process fully described symbolically in "The Secret Symbols of the Rosicrucians of the 16th and 17th Century,"[1] a book easily comprehensible if studied by the light of wisdom, but unintelligible for the carnal mind, that sees all truths perverted. Some explanations have also been attempted in the book entitled "In the Pronaos of the Temple."[2] We will only say that there the *Three Substances* appear as the *Three Beginnings;* the first manifestation of the Unity as a Trinity, and the Seven *Tattwas* as the seven primitive spirits,[3] or "living breaths" issuing from the bosom of Parabrahm.[4]

The Universe is the *Macrocosm,* and Man the *Microcosm,* and as the first great Cause is the creator of the world and the cause of all evolution, so is individual man the creator in his own interior and external world, capable of causing certain superior states in his mind by the power of his will in obedience to the law, and to create forms by means of his thoughts, while the condition of his interior state will in time produce corresponding effects and transmutation in his physical body. Well will it pay him to devote all his time to this practice of Alchemy and obtain the pure gold of wisdom from the inferior metals represented by his animal passions. These passions are the capital lent to him by nature to make them into "silver and

[1] Occult Publ. Co., Boston, Mass; and Theosoph. Publ. Soc., London.
[2] Occult Publ. Co., Boston, Mass.; and Theosoph. Publ. Soc., London.
[3] *Jacob Boehme.*
[4] "Secret Doctrine," Vol. I., p. 106.

gold," while he lives upon this earth: they are the steps upon which he can climb up to immortality and find his own true divine Self.

To practise this kind of Alchemy he will require no books, no furnaces and no tools; for he is himself the alembic, the fire and the substance to be ennobled. There, in his silent laboratory and with doors closed against all vain and carnal desires and selfish thoughts, he may *mortify* his terrestrial nature by gaining the victory of self-control, so that his higher nature may become *liberated* from animal bonds by entering into the *resurrection* from the tomb of ignorance into the light of self-knowledge. To accomplish this he will have to *purify* his mind and let his soul become *animated* by the power of the spirit of truth; that which is inert in him must become *sublimated* in the fire of divine love, so as to rise to heaven in the shape of holy aspirations, while the smoke of sophistry, dogmatism, false science and self-righteousness must be permitted to pass out through the chimney, to return no more. In this way will he be able to find the way of combining ☿ with ♂ and thus to make it into substantial gold that will last through eternity.

The above will be sufficient to give a hint in regard to the character of Alchemy and its relation to chemistry. Between these two aspects there is a third one, namely, what may be called "Astral Alchemy."

The Alchemy of the Astral Plane.—As the lower Alchemy requires for its practice the faculties of the physical body, and the celestial Alchemy the energy of the spirit having become a power in the body of man: so the practice of Alchemy in dealing with that which belongs to the astral plane requires the evolution of consciousness and perception in the astral organism of man; for in the majority of those who live on the physical plane, the astral form is as unconscious of its surroundings upon the plane to which it belongs, and as ignorant of their nature, as a babe is ignorant of the meanings of things in this world. It is, however, not our purpose to enter into this subject, as this would bring us into the almost inexhaustible realm of spiritism, hypnotism, witchcraft and sorcery: all of which things are superstitions if believed in by those who know nothing about their laws, but realities for those who know the laws by which such phenomena take place.[1] The key to the understanding of these phenomena is in the realization of the truth that the Universe is a manifestation of power upon the three planes of existence. The spiritual plane has its seven states of existence, representing self-conscious intelligent powers, thrones and dominions, angels and archangels, all of these being manifestations of the primordial cause called *God.* The physical plane has its seven states of existence, represented as powers in which consciousness is still latent. In the *middle region,* the astral plane, we also find again seven states of existence in the form of living forces attaining consciousness in the organization of man. There the "seven planets" manifest themselves either for good or for evil according to the nature of the person in whom they become manifest. Thus, for instance, that universal element which is symbolized as ♀ will become manifested in man as universal love or as selfishness according to his condition. If   ♀ rules his ♂ he will have self-control; but if his ♂ rules his love, he will give way to his lusts. If the element of ♄ in him rules his ☾, his intelligence will be of a terrestrial nature belonging to the spirit of the earth; but if his intelligence is master over his earthly elements, he will be capable of high aspirations. If the element of ☿ rules his ♃, he will employ his intellect for the purpose of satisfying his greed, but if ♃ is the master of his ☿ he will be of a noble character.

All this is merely said to hint at the sublimity of alchemical science and call attention to the universal truth; that *every principle, in whatever plane of existence it may exist, is not a product of the form in which it develops and manifests itself; but that the form is the field for its development and manifestation;* in the same sense as the universal) sunlight is not a product of the bodies upon which it shines, but the bodies are instruments for the development and manifestation of the qualities of light. Thus the life, consciousness, will, virtue, passion, or any other spiritual, emotional, or physical state of a man is not the product

---

[1] "Superstition"—from *super*=over and *sto*=to stand—is a belief in the knowledge of the attributes of a thing, while these attributes are beyond our conception. A superstition is therefore a misconception of an existing thing, or a creation of fancy: an erroneous conclusion arrived at by the observation of a phenomenon, without an understanding of the law which produced the phenomenon.

of his form, but a manifestation of a universal life principle becoming manifested in him according to the conditions presented by his constitution. Life is only one, manifesting itself in animals as animal life, in plants as vegetable life, etc. Consciousness is only one, manifesting itself as true self-consciousness in spiritual beings, and as instincts in the lower animal kingdom. Love is only one and universal, otherwise it could not manifest everywhere the same qualities; it does not belong to one individual or one country; it is born in heaven; but it becomes manifest upon the earth in men, animals, plants and minerals, under different aspects according to the conditions which it finds. Everything is a manifestation of one primordial Unity revealing itself in a threefold aspect. Man himself is nothing more than a manifestation of the universal power that called him into existence and built up his bodily form. He is not his body nor his mind; but the expression upon a lower plane of a higher individual state of being; one of the letters that constitute the great alphabet of humanity. Being continually deluded by the illusion caused by the apparent isolation of his form and its separation from other forms of existence, he imagines himself to be something essentially separated from other beings, and thus he forgets his own universal nature. Only when man begins to realise what he himself in reality is, can he begin to attain real knowledge in regard to three kingdoms of Nature. The object of science is said to be the recognition of truth, but it is also self-evident that no true science can exist as long as the truth is not recognised and even rejected; for nothing less than by the power of truth in man can the truth be known. No man can have self-knowledge of anything which is not within himself.

It will be clear that this subject is so vast as to render it impossible, in a work of this kind, to do more than merely skim over the surface, and a thousand things have to remain unsaid which ought to be explained; but it is not our purpose to enter into the details of the science of the *Astronomy of Life* or the *Chemistry of Life,* or to discuss at length the highest problems of *Occult Philosophy.* The object of the present work is merely to remove existing misconceptions, and to throw out seeds, which, if they fall upon a fruitful ground, will grow and bear fruits, such as ripen not in the outer shell of Nature, but within her inner temple, in the higher regions of thought.

IV. THE VIRTUE OF THE PHYSICIAN.

"Virtue" means *power;* it is said to be derived from *vir,* Man, and means manly power, efficacy, strength. Man being some-what more than a physical body or an animal, it means a superior, spiritual, substantial power, such as becomes mani-fested as nobility of character, purity of heart, clearness of mind, strength of will, firmness of decision, quickness of perception, penetration of thought, benevolence, kindness, honesty, truth-fulness, unselfishness, modesty. This virtue is something infinitely superior to the common "virtuosity," which consists in an outward appearing of being virtuous and pious for fear of exposure and dread of criticism, and it is also infinitely superior to what is called "morality" by the moralists; a thing praised as the highest attainable object; but being in fact nothing more than a conforming to certain customs and views. There is not necessarily any self-sacrifice in practising morals, but it is more often a means for gratifying one's vanity. The word "moral" comes from *mores,* manners. What is according to the manners and customs in one country, and therefore regarded as *"moral"* there, is immoral in another place where different manners exist. A morality without spirituality is of no real value. The same may be said of "ethics," derived from *ēthos,* custom, and which seems to be one of the terms that have been invented for the purpose of creating confusion, and avoiding calling spiritual things by their right names.

The *virtue* which, according to Paracelsus, is the fourth pillar of the temple of Medicine, has nothing to do with shams; it means *the power resulting from being a man in the true sense of this term and being in possession of not merely the theories regarding the treatment of Disease but of the power to cure them oneself.*

There are at present thousands of medical practitioners, whose only merit is and ever will be, that they have succeeded in passing an examination and obtaining the title M.D.; but the title "doctor" means merely an academical degree; the diploma merely certifies that the examiners believe the student to have fulfilled all that the regulations require, and although such a title may involve the right to poison and kill without being punished for it, the conferring of such a degree does not constitute a physician. The true physician as well as the real priest is ordained by God. Paracelsus says in substance as follows:—

"He who can cure disease is a physician. Neither emperors nor popes, neither colleges nor high schools can create physicians. They can confer privileges and cause a person who is not a physician to appear as if he were one; they can give him permission to kill, but they cannot give him the power to cure; they cannot make him a real physician if he has not already been ordained by God. The true physician does not brag about his cleverness or praise his medicines or seek to monopolize the right of robbing the patient; for he knows that the work must praise the master, and not the master the work. There is a knowledge which is derived from man, and another knowledge which is derived from God through the light of nature. He who has not been born to be a physician will never succeed. A physician should be faithful and charitable. He who loves only himself and his own pocket will be of little benefit to the sick. Medicine is much more an art than a science. To know the experience of others is useful to a physician; but all the learning of books cannot make a man a physician, unless he is one by nature. Medical wisdom is only given by God." (Comp. "Paragranum," i. 4.)

This virtue which constitutes the true physician cannot be created by colleges, nor can it be conferred by anyone personally upon himself. No one can confer upon himself a thing which he does not possess, or without the aid of any higher influence make himself better than that which he is; because, as has been explained above, the power exercised by any form is not the creation of the form, but an eternal principle, entering into objective existence in forms and becoming manifested in and through them by its own power. Neither truth nor wisdom can be manufactured; they exist independently of all opinions, observations, speculation, and logic; they may be hidden from our sight like the sun on a rainy day; but as the sun is independent of our being aware of his presence, so the truth exists eternally whether or not it is acknowledged by us. If the whole generation of mankind at present walking this earth should turn into idiots, the truth would not therefore cease to be, but would become manifested again as wisdom in a more enlightened age.

Nothing can rise to heaven but what has descended from it, we can only by overcoming that which is false render ourselves receptive for that which is true. *Eckhart* says:—"Divine Wisdom is to God what the sunlight is to the sun; it is one with Him, a necessary activity, a never dying fountain, having its source in the heart of God."

This brings us back again to a *religious* basis (if we are permitted to use this ill-treated and misunderstood term), and to the necessity that he who makes it his profession to employ the laws of nature and treat the body of man should know the position which man occupies in nature and the position which nature occupies in regard to the origin from which it originates.

This science requires not mere words, but self-knowledge. Wisdom can only be taught by Wisdom itself; but a science based upon a recognition of truth disperses the clouds which prevent the light of the truth from entering into the heart and becoming incorporated and manifested in man.

III.
THE FIVE CAUSES OF DISEASE.

IF we inquire from modern medical science: What are the causes of diseases? we shall probably be answered:

1. *Age.* 2. *Heredity.* 3. *Intermarriage.* 4. *Sex.* 5. *Tempera-ment.* 6. *Climate and locality.* 7. *Town or country.* 8. *Hygienic conditions.* 9. *Occupation.* 10. *Air.* 11. *Previous disease.* 12. *Mental and moral conditions.* 13. *External physical conditions.* 14. *Poisons.* 15. *Temperature.* 16. *Diet.* 17. *Epidemic disease, contagion, malaria, parasites and growths.*[1]

We will forbear to pass any remarks upon this classification of the causes of diseases, which merely enumerates certain conditions in which diseases may arise, and we will pass on to the classification of the causes of diseases given by Paracelsus; but as this subject has already received attention in a previously published work on the doctrines of Paracelsus[2], the following is intended merely to supply additional food for thought.

Paracelsus says:

"All diseases have a beginning in either of the three substances;[3] Salt, Sulphur, or Mercury; which means that they may take their origin either within the kingdom of matter, within the realm of the soul, or in the sphere of the spirit. If body, soul and mind are in perfect harmony with each other, no disharmony exists; but if a cause of discord arises in either one of these three planes, it communicates itself to the rest."

Before proceeding further we will inquire about the nature of these *three Substances:*

SALT ⊖, SULPHUR ♁, AND MERCURY ☿,

which may be translated as Matter, Energy and Intelligence. They are in fact not three essentially different things, but only three modes of activity of one and the same thing; for everything is substantial, each contains a latent or active force, in each is the potentiality of consciousness, if it has not already become manifested therein. Everything exists, therefore, by reason of these "three substances," and if we for the sake of forming some

---

[1] *Richard Quain,* "Dictionary of Medicine," 1883.
[2] " Paracelsus." (London: Trübner and Co., 1887.)
[3] The word "substance" comes from *sub,* under, and *sto,* to stand, and means the principle underlying phenomenal existence, the basis of the manifestation of power. It is only too customary to give to such terms a wrong interpretation, and then to fight the man of straw created by oneself.

idea of their nature look at the world as a manifestation of *electricity* (which must necessarily be substantial, as there could be no force without substance), we may compare them as follows:

⊖ to electric resistance.
♃ to the tension of electromotive force.
☿ to the intensity of the current.

No one would ever think of these three measures as being separate entities, which like "substance, energy and intelligence" are merely three aspects or conceptions of one universal life; but these distinctions are necessary for the purpose of forming a conception.

"Nothing can be thoroughly known without a knowledge of its beginning. Man is placed into *three substances,* in each of which he has a beginning; and each thing has its substance, its number and measure (constituting their harmony). From (the state of) these three substances originate all causes, origins, and also the understanding of diseases. These three substances, *Sulphur, Mercurius, Sal,* give to everything its corporeality, each substance having its own qualities. If these qualities are good (in harmony with each other) there will be no disease but if they enter into opposition to each other, disease (disharmony) will be the result. (*Paracelsus,* "Paramirum," *Lib.* I., 1, 2, and 3)."

Within these three kingdoms disorders may arise from either of the following *five causes of disease:*

1. From the *Ens astrale;* namely from surrounding conditions in external nature.

2. From the *Ens veneni;* meaning from poisons and impurities.

3. From the *Ens naturæ;* including causes inherited from the parents.

4. From the *Ens spirituale;* especially those caused by an evil will or morbid imagination.

5. From the *Ens Dei;* to which belong the ills arising from evil *Karma* acquired during this or a previous incarnation; in other words, the result of *divine justice.*

We will now attempt to define the meaning of these five beginnings.

I.—ENS ASTRALE.[1]

Diseases arising from external influences; whether from physical nature or from deeper causes; the planet upon which we live being itself an *astrum* (star), having a physical and ethereal body, a life, a soul, a mind and a spirit.

"The stars on the sky do not form a man. Man grows out of two beginnings; the *Ens seminis* (the male sperm) and the *Ens virtutis* (the reincarnating spiritual monad). He has therefore two natures, a corporeal and a spiritual nature, and either of these two requires its *digest* (*matrix* and nutriment). As the womb of the mother is the world surrounding the child, from which the foetus receives its nutriment, so is terrestrial nature from which the terrestrial body of man receives the influences acting in his organism. The *Ens astrale* is a thing which we do not see, but which contains us and everything that lives and has sensation. It is that which contains the air, and from which and in which live all the elements, and which we symbolize as M *(Mysterium).* "Paramirum," *Lib.* I.)

This *Ens Astrorum* is therefore evidently the *Akâsa,* which forms the basis of all material things in physical nature, and if the close relation between man's physical nature and the physical nature surrounding him were better known, it would become more comprehensible how the states of the all-penetrating ether, changes in temperature, heat and cold, electric and magnetic conditions in nature, come to affect the physical nature of man, acting internally by inducing corresponding changes in his microcosm, even if he is protected against the direct action of rain, storm, moisture, cold, heat, etc., etc. A sudden change of conditions in the outside air can affect a patient imprisoned in a room where no such change is perceptible, and a cloudy day produce a melancholy effect even upon a blind person. There are no end of diseases which for want of a better explanation are attributed to "catching cold," etc., while in fact it is the existence of certain conditions in the all-pervading ether, which induces similar conditions in the body of the patient. Thus, for instance, changes of the moon, or the position of the moon, or the magnetic currents of the earth, produce certain effects in certain persons, even if these persons know nothing about these laws, for it is a fact well known to the ancients, but which has almost been lost sight of by modern medicine, that man, apart from the order in which his organs are arranged, is essentially a counterpart of nature, an image of the

---

[1] *"Ens"* means a beginning.

38

world on a smaller scale, a *microcosm* within the macrocosm. An atmospheric pressure in outside nature produces an atmospheric pressure in him; if nature rejoices in the sunlight of spring, his heart rejoices with it; if storms rage on the outside, similar storms may he aroused in him, etc., etc. He is, in fact, only a laboratory in which the universal forces of nature are performing their work. To this chapter also belong all miasmas and contagious influences, with all the bacteriæ, microbes, amœbæ, bacilli, etc., etc., which are the pride of modern discoverers, but whose characteristics, if not the forms of their bodies, were well known to Paracelsus, who describes them under the names of *Talpa, Matena, Tortilleos, Permates,* etc. He says:

"God has caused living creatures to exist in all the elements, and there is nothing empty of life. That which becomes manifested in the visible kingdom has come into existence by being generated in the upper regions. Without such a generation above, it could not have become manifested below." ("Lib. Meteorum," I. 4.)

Since the modern discovery of the cholera, tubercle bacilli, and other micro-organisms spreading contagious diseases, it has been the opinion of many, that the presence of such microbes was the only and fundamental cause of such diseases; but still more recent investigations have shown such that the presence of these microbes does not constitute the whole cause; for they have been with impunity introduced into the human organism, and have also been found to exist in persons who had fully recovered from such a disease. This surely shows that there must be an influence causing the microbes to come into existence, after which they can spread and multiply if the conditions are favourable, and the fundamental cause of such epidemics is therefore not the presence of the microbes, this being merely a symptom, but the influences which cause them to come into existence, producing *states* of which the bodies of these organisms are a product and expression and which appears to proceed from causes situated deeper than visible physical nature, if we do not mistake the form for the "spirit" of which the form is the symbol.

"Human science knows how to philosophize about the things that come within its external observation; but Wisdom shows what is contained in the *Prima Materia,* which is a greater and higher knowledge than that of the *Ultima Materia* (the physical plane)."

("Meteorum," I. 4.)

This "higher region," from which such injurious influences originate, causing the growth of miasmas and microbes, is the *"astral plane,"* or the soul of the world, and as the evil states in the soul of the world are caused by the evil states of the human mind, it becomes comprehensible how epidemic diseases, pestilence and plague, no less than wars, are the ultimate results of disharmonies and depraved spiritual states in the soul of humanity. The greatest truth if seen through a perverted mind appears distorted as a caricature and superstition; it can be seen in its own light, only if properly understood.

The astral plane is the plane of desires, emotions, and passions; that is to say, the plane of those influences (forms of the universal will), which become manifested as desires, emotions, and passions in the animal organism, and if we were to enter this subject, it would bring us within the realm of the supersensual but nevertheless actual kingdom of living elemental powers belonging to the soul of the world. If our eyes were opened to the perception of thoughts, it would be seen how a continual thought-transference is taking place among individual minds, influencing and determining their actions, even if they are not aware of it, causing not only individual moral diseases, insanities, obsessions and crimes, but whole epidemics of such kinds. There is an immense field for investigation for the psychologist; not for that kind of "psychologists" who imagine that insanity is under all circumstances a disturbance of the functions of the brain from physical causes, but for those who can realise that the functions of the brain may be disturbed by the disordered action of the mind; for although in many cases of brain disease it is as difficult to determine whether the disorder of the mind or that of the brain existed first, as it would he to answer the question, which existed first, the hen or the egg? nevertheless a lesion of the tissues of the brain does not take place without a cause, and this cause in the majority of such cases comes from the sphere of the emotions and thoughts.

If there is no mind, there can be no mental disease. If mind is something (even if it were, as some imagine, the product of the physiological function of the brain), it must be something substantial, and being something substantial, it is able to produce substantial effects; moreover, its actions show a certain order and harmony, which go to prove that mind has an organisation. If this order and harmony be disturbed, discord, disease, insanity will be the result. Without the presence of mind nothing would come into existence; without the consciousness in the All, no brain would be able to manifest consciousness, and this is what Paracelsus means when he says:—

"Whatever exists upon this earth, also exists in the *firmament* (space). God does not make clothes for men, but he gives them a tailor. (Forms do not grow by accident; but they are the ultimate result of the action of the constructive power in nature.) The essence of things is hidden in space; existing invisibly in the *firmament,* and impressing itself upon material substances, when it becomes visible by entering within our sphere of perception." ("Meteorum," I. 4.)

Thus we have in the *Ens Astrale* a field in which exist the causes of numerous kinds of diseases; the thorough understanding of which requires a still deeper penetration into the secrets of nature and a higher conception of its constitution than is at present presented by the natural sciences of this day.

II.—ENS VENENI.

Diseases originating from poisonous actions and impurities in all three planes of existence.

Nothing is poisonous or impure if it stands by itself, only if two things whose natures are incompatible with each other come into contact, can a poisonous action take place or an impure condition be produced.

"Everything is in itself perfect and good. Only when it enters into relation with another thing does relative good and evil come into existence. If anything enters into the constitution of man, which is not in harmony with its elements, the one is to the other an impurity, and can become a poison." ("Paramirum," II. I.)

There is no doubt that modern chemistry, physiology and pathology teach more than ancient science in regard to the chemical constitution, the physiological action of poisons and of the pathological) effects which they produce in the animal body; but to explain the order in which a process takes place is not sufficient to explain why it takes place, and there is still a wide field open for investigation; for at present we can only record the fact that certain physical substances have a destructive action upon the human body; while the same substances with a little difference in the arrangements of their molecules, are not only not injurious, but even used as food;[1] that certain substances have a specific action upon the emotional nature in man, causing an inclination to certain states of his astral constitution, such as irritability of temper, anger, cupidity, etc., which they could not have if no corresponding elements were contained in them; while others have a specific action upon the mind, such as the fading of memory, paralysis of the will, excitement of the imagination, all of which they could not accomplish if no substantial mind principle existed in them.

To material science the universe is a product of mechanical force created by unconscious matter; to the idealist it is a dream which has nothing real in it; but seen with the eye of wisdom it is a manifestation of life, with the potentiality of consciousness contained in everything. Love and hate exist in minerals as they do in men, only in another state of consciousness, and a tragedy or comedy might be written in regard to their family history; describing, for instance, how the beautiful Princess Sodium fell in love and was married to a fiery youth called Oxygen, and how the happy union lasted until one day a jealous knight, named Chlorine, fell in love with her, and although he himself was married to a flighty woman whose name was Hydrogenia, he abducted the princess, and there was nothing left for poor Oxygen but to take the deserted woman and turn to water with her. Such a story would differ from a similar one enacted in human life only in so far as the actors in the latter would intelligently and consciously follow certain laws which are enacted without individual intelligence in the mineral kingdom. There is only one Consciousness and one law of Harmony in the world, and according to it accords and discords arise in all the three kingdoms of nature.

The influence of the light of the truth is a poison to the erroneous conceptions existing within the mind, and earthly thoughts are impurities to the mind that aspires to the kingdom of heaven. Evil desires create evil thoughts and give birth to evil

---

[1] It is hardly necessary to furnish examples, such as, for instance, presented by Strychnine, composed of $C_{21} H_{22} N_2 O_2$, a very poisonous substance; while the same elements combined in a different proportion are contained as gluten in our food. If we accept the theory of vibration, which appears as a necessary result of the universe being substance in motion, the cause of such secrets will easily be found in the discords existing between the vibrations constituting these substances. This theory of harmony will also explain why certain chemicals combine with others in certain proportions.

acts; good acts procreate their species, giving rise to good thoughts and aspirations, from which good children are born. The sum of men's individual desires constitutes the desires of the soul of the world; the sum of the thoughts and opinions of mankind constitutes the mental atmosphere by which the world in general, and each locality in particular, is surrounded; and the state of the mind ultimately expresses itself upon the outward plane of manifestation. It is not more difficult to poison a mind with impure thoughts than to poison a body with drugs. Impure is he who has many diverging desires, pure is the mind having only one will.

Popular medicine deals only with external effects and physical causes, occult science goes deeper, seeking for fundamental causes and final effects, which are of far greater importance than the passing manifestations taking place in the physical form. Thus, for instance, a promiscuous sexual intercourse not only causes venereal diseases; but as during that act a commingling of the inner natures takes place to a certain extent, a man cohabiting with a depraved woman takes on some of her characteristics and joins to a certain extent her future *Karma* and destiny to his own. The basis of the existence of human beings is what, for want of a better expression, has been called the *Will* (Spirit or Life), and as one body may colour or poison another, likewise a colouring, and perhaps poisoning, takes place by a blending of spirit during sexual intercourse; this "spiritual substance" being the essence of each human being.

"If a woman leaves her husband, she is then not free from him, nor he from her; for a marital union having once been established, remains a union for all eternity." ("De Homunculis.")

That which nourishes a thing, goes to make up its substance. The physical body receives its nutriment from the physical plane, the soul is nourished by the influences coming from the soul of the world, the intellect is nourished, grows and expands in the intellectual plane; an ill-fed body becomes diseased; a soul living on morbid desires and inordinate longings becomes depraved, a mind fed with false theories, errors and superstitions becomes dwarfed, perverted and unable to turn its face towards the sunlight of truth. The food for soul and mind is as substantial to them as material food is substantial to the material body; body, soul, and spirit being three states of the eternal *One,* manifested on three different planes of existence, being governed by only one fundamental law. What the stomach is in the body, the memory is in the mind. Both are related together; a dyspeptic stomach causes a defective memory and an irritable mind; an irritable temperament causes indigestion and forgetfulness; forgetfulness can cause inattention, irritability and dyspepsia. Soul, body and mind are one in man, and disorders existing in one can cause impurities in the other; each passion in man, each superstition in which he firmly believes, is capable of poisoning his body and of producing a certain disease. A belief in salvation made easy renders a man indolent, indolence causes want of self-control, which causes want of resistance to injurious influences in the physical plane. Repeated physical misfortunes may make a man a coward, and his cowardliness prevents him from letting go of a doctrine which he intuitively known to be false. Anger is not only injurious to bodily health, but drives away reason by confusing the mind; wrath causes not only mental but also physical shortsightedness, and hard-hearing is often the only cause of a suspicious character.

Thus innumerable comparisons may be drawn and analogies be found, and cases cited to prove the correctness of this theory, if our space would permit it, and if it were necessary to prove by arguments and facts the truth of the unity of the all, which must be self-evident to everyone taking the trouble to seek for the answer to such questions within himself.

But the highest cannot act upon the lowest without an intermediary link connecting them; the spirit cannot act upon the body without the connecting link of the soul, nor the soul upon the body except by means of the life. We cannot cook a dish of soup for a starving beggar by means of the fire of love; but love moves the will and induces actions which the mind directs, and thus the soup may be cooked after all owing to the power of love or charity. The greatest difficulty in the understanding of occult laws arises from the circumstance that we cannot perceive remote causes or seek to connect them with ultimate effects without being able to see through the intricate network of intermediary causes between the two ends.

III.—ENS NATURAE.

Diseases which have their origin in certain conditions inherent in the constitution of man.

Man is a perfect child of nature. There is not a single essence in his constitution which does not exist in nature; neither is there any substance or power to be found in nature which does not exist in him, either actually or potentially, undeveloped or developed.

"There are many who say that man is a *microcosm;* but few understand what this really means. As the world is itself an organism with all its constellations, so is man a constellation (organism), a world in itself, and as the firmament (space) of the world is ruled by no creature, so the firmament which is within man (his mind) is not subject to any other creature. This firmament (sphere of mind) in man has its planets and stars (mental states), its exaltations, conjunctions and oppositions (states of feelings, thoughts, emotions, ideas, loves and hates), call them by whatever name you like, and as all the celestial bodies in space are connected with each other by invisible links, so are the organs in man not entirely independent of each other, but depend on each other to a certain extent. His heart is ☉, his brain his ☽, the spleen his ♄, the liver ♃, the lungs ☿, and the kidneys ♀." ("Paramirum," III. 4.)

Man has two kinds of natures. His physical organism is a product of that nature which he received from his terrestrial parents; his mental organisation is the result of a higher and quite different kind of evolution. His terrestrial nature includes not only his visible organism, but also the organisation of his astral form and his mental constitution.

"There are two kinds of flesh. The flesh of *Adam* (the physical body) is gross earthly flesh; the flesh that is *derived from Adam* is of a subtle kind. It is not made of gross matter, it penetrates through all walls without requiring doors or holes; nevertheless both kinds of flesh have their blood and bones, and both differ again from the spirit." *(Paracelsus, "De Nymphis.")*

Man having within himself the same essences and powers, and there being only one universal law of evolution, there takes place in him a development similar to, if not identical with, the development in eternal and internal nature. Accords and discords in his nature can grow and swell into harmonies or disharmonies, and constitute the whole man a symphony or cacophony, colouring his whole being and transmitting this to his offspring. A seed of wheat and a seed of barley resemble each other, and nevertheless wheat grows out of one and barley out of the other. The *ovum* of a human being shows no essential difference from that of a monkey; nevertheless out of the one grows a human being and out of the other a monkey. The nature of man is fully

45

expressed in every part of his organism, and in the sperm of the father is contained not only the quality of this or that part of his nature, but the potentiality of the whole.[1]

The quality of the constitution of a man determines the length of his natural life.

"If a child is born, its *firmament* (astral body and mind, etc.) is born with it, containing the seven principles, of which each has its own potencies and qualities. What is called *'predestination'* is only the quality of the powers in man. The weakness or strength of his constitution determines whether his life is to be short or long, according to natural laws; the planets in him run their course whether he has a long or a short life, only in the former case the course of his planets is of a longer, and in the other case of a shorter duration. The quality of the constitution which a man receives at his birth determines the length of his natural life, just as the quantity of sand in an hour glass determines the time when it will have run down." ("Paramirum," L. I., Tr. iii., C. 5.)

The *Ens Naturae* therefore refers to those beginnings in man's constitution which are the result of the quality of his body, soul and mind as he received them from nature, and includes all inherited physical diseases, qualities of temperament and mental peculiarities; for the earthly part of the mind *(Kâma Mamas)* belongs to terrestrial nature and its tendencies are inherited; while the spiritual part of the mind *(Mamas Buddhi)* is not inherited from the parents, but belongs to the spiritual man whose parent exists in eternity.[2]

This class includes all internal diseases originating from disorders arising among the interaction of the physiological functions of the organs of the body, or of the interaction between these and those of the soul (the emotions) and mind (thoughts).

---

[1] In the recognition of the law is contained the key to the understanding of chiromancy, phrenology, physiognomy, psychometry, etc., and their value in practising medicine; for although the physical form, owing to external physical conditions, may not be an exact image of the internal nature of man, nevertheless the character of the mind is to a certain extent impressed visibly upon each part of the body, and being a whole and a unity, the whole of that character may be read in every part of the body, if we know how to read it; in the same sense as a botanist can tell the character of a tree by examining one of its leaves, for he knows at once to what class of trees it belongs.

[2] "The character of a man and his talents, aptitude, dexterity, etc., are not given to him by (terrestrial) nature. His spirit is not a product of nature, but comes from the incorporeal realm. You should not say that he receives these things from nature; the sages never said so." ("Paramirum," L. I., Tr. iii., C. 2.)

This system of Paracelsus includes the whole realm of modern physiology and pathology; but it penetrates deeper, for it investigates the functions of soul and mind, and follows the development of an evil desire or thought until it ultimately finds its expression in an external manifestation of visible pathological states. To enter into the details of this field of pathology is not possible within the limits of this book.

There is no indication that the sympathies and antipathies, in other words the physiological relations existing between the different organs in the human body, are better known at the present time than they were at the time of Paracelsus: on the contrary, he speaks of the currents of the life-principle taking place between these organs, while modern anatomy speaks only of nerves, which are in regard to the "life-fluid" what electric wires are in regard to electricity.

"The heart sends its spirit (will power) through the whole of the body, as the sun his power to all the planets and earths; the ☾ (the intelligence of the brain) goes to the heart and back again to the brain. The fire (heat) takes its origin in the (chemical) activity of the organs (the lungs), but pervades the whole body. The *liquor vitæ* (essence of life) is universally distributed and moves (circulates) in the body. This 'humor' contains many different powers, and cause in him 'metals' (virtues or vices) of various kinds." ("Paramirum," L. I.. Tr. 3.)

In regard to this subject modern medical science says:—

"A wide basis of positive knowledge in regard to this subject does not exist. The physiology of the different departments of the sympathetic system of nerves is now only beginning to shape itself, while on the side of pathology and morbid anatomy there is even still less of definite knowledge. Thus it happens that for the most part only conjectures, often very insecurely based are current, or can be said to exist in regard to the dependence of definite sets of symptoms, or distinct diseases, upon disordered actions or morbid changes occurring in one or other part of the sympathetic system of nerves." ("H. Charlton Bastian.")

Both ancient and modern science are right as far as they go; only while modern science pays all of its attention to the forms (organs, nerves, etc.), which are merely the products of certain principles and powers and the instruments for their activity, ancient science deals with these powers themselves, taking only into secondary consideration the visible instruments in and through which they become manifest. Modern science, so to say, studies the muscular movements of a musician, occult science knows the art of music itself. Material science is the servant mixing the paints for the painter; the true physician is the artist who knows how to paint. The one studies the tools which the workman uses; the other sees also the workman himself. These comparisons are not drawn for the purpose of throwing discredit upon modern medical science, nor for the purpose of blaming any modern physician for not employing powers which he does not possess; but for the purpose of indicating that a knowledge of physical phenomena and visible forms is not the limit of all attainable knowledge, and that there exists a higher and more important kind of knowledge, based upon a higher perception, such as is attained only through the higher development of the spiritual character of man; which becomes possible only when earthly presumption and vanity are overcome and when, by stepping up higher, he realises the nothingness of the terrestrial illusion of "self."

IV.—ENS SPIRITUALE.
Diseases arising from spiritual causes.

"Spirit"—from *spiro,* to blow—means breath. "Breath means a power, quite distinct from mechanical force, as being endowed with consciousness, life and intelligence. In its aspect as an universal power, it means the breath of God which caused the universe to come from a subjective state into objective existence; in its individual aspect it means the spiritual power dwelling in man.[1]

Spirit is Consciousness in every plane of existence; but from this it does not follow that all the forms in which it dwells necessarily manifest self-consciousness or are even conscious of existence. For the manifestation of perfect spiritual self-consciousness a spiritual organism is required, such as an average man does not possess, if he has not been reborn in the spirit. In the forms of the mineral kingdom the presence of spirit is perceptible by the manifestations of mineral life, in the vegetable kingdom by the manifestations of vegetable life, and in the animal kingdom by those of animal life, for spirit is itself the basis of life in the physical, astral, intellectual and spiritual world; and as the spirit of the universe is the spiritual breath of

---

[1] "Then shall the dust return to earth as it was, and the spirit shall return to God who gave it," ("Ecclesiastes," xii., 7.)

God, issuing from the centre and returning to it, so is the spirit of man the spiritual power which enters into his constitution, and issues again when the body dies.

"That is a spirit, which is born from our thoughts; immaterial and in the living body. That which is born after our death is the soul." ("Paramirum," L. I., C. iv., 2.)

"The spirit is not born from reasoning, but from the will." (*Ibid. 3.*)

"Spirit," in other words, is a form of *Will* endowed with thought; a spiritual power, neither good nor evil in itself; but which becomes good or evil according to the purpose for which it is employed. Its functions are willing, imagining, and remembering.

A great deal has been written about the power of will and imagination in Nature, by means of which the types existing in the memory of the universal mind continually find re-expression in physical visible forms;[1] in this place we have to deal only with the qualities of these three functions, and the effects which they produce in the body of man.

In the previous three divisions of this chapter we have had under our consideration causes of diseases originating in the terrestrial part of the human constitution; this and the following deals with his spiritual part.

"There are two subjects in man, one is a material, the other a spiritual being (thought-body), impalpable, invisible, subject to its own diseases (discords); one belonging to the material, the other to the spiritual world, each having its own states of consciousness, perception and memory, its own associations with beings of its kind. Nevertheless, both are one during this life, and the spirit influences the body; but not the body the spirit. Therefore if the spirit is diseased, it is of no use to doctor the body; but if the body is diseased; it can be cured by administering remedies to the spirit." *(Lib.* "Paramir.," I., iv., 4 and 7.)

This spiritual part, or the thought body of man, is the vehicle for the reincarnating spirit, when the spiritual individuality evolves a new personality upon the earth. For the purpose of understanding what is said in the following division of this chapter, it will be necessary to understand the theory of *Reincarnation,* of which we can only present an outline within the space of this work. H. P. Blavatsky says that which reincarnates is:

"The Spiritual thinking Ego, the permanent principle in man, or

---

[1] See: "Magic, white and black," "Paracelsus," "Boehme," etc.

that which is the seat of the Manas. It is not ATMA, *or even* ATMA-
BUDDHI, *which is the individual or divine man, but* MANAS; *for Atman
is the Universal All, and becomes the Higher Self of man only in
conjunction with* BUDDHI, *its vehicle, which links* IT *to the individuality
(or the divine Man).* "[1]

The resurrection of the physical body is a modern superstition in which none of the ancient philosophers or real
Christians ever believed.[2]

Will.

"Will" comes from *willan,* desire; but is quite distinct from
that selfish desire which is the result of the fancies of the brain;
the true will is a strong power which comes from the centre, the
heart, and in its highest aspect it is that creative power which
called the world into existence. All the voluntary and
involuntary actions in nature and in the organism of man
originate in the action of will, whether or not we are conscious
of it.

"You do not know a tithe of the real power of the will." (*Paracelsus,* "Paramir.," I., iv., 8.)

Upon the physical plane the will acts, so to say, unconsciously, carrying out blindly the laws of nature, causing
attractions, repulsions, guiding the mechanical, chemical and
physiological functions of the body without man's intelligence
taking any part in the process. Man is himself a manifestation of
will, and the will (spirit) in him can perform many things
without depending on the intellectual activity of the brain; all of
which is left unexplained by modern physiology, although it
cannot deny the facts. Thus an experienced pianist does not
require to determine first which movement he should give to the
muscles of his fingers before striking a key; but he does this

---

[1] "Key to Theosophy," p. 121 (London, 1889).
[2] "There is an invisible organism in man, not placed within the *three substances;*
a body which (unlike the material one) does not come from the *Limbus* (matter)
but has its origin in the living breath of God. It is not a body coming into
existence after death, to rise up on the judgment day; for the physical body being
a nonentity (unreal) cannot become resurrected after death, neither shall we be
called upon to give account about our physical health and disease; but we shall
be judged according to the things that have issued from our will. This spiritual
body in man is the flesh that comes from the breath of God. There are two
bodies, but only one flesh." ("Paramir.," *Lib.* II., 8.)

instinctively after his spirit has been educated to it. Rope-walking, gymnastic feats and acts of all kinds are the products of a trained will, and would be impossible without that. They may be superintended by the intellect, but are not guided by it. Its sphere of action is limited to that of the body in which it dwells.

In its higher aspect the will is a conscious power, manifesting itself as emotions, virtues and vices of various kinds. Its sphere of action extends as far as the sphere of the influence of the individual mind. Thus the will of a superior person exercises an influence over his inferiors, a teacher over his pupils, a general over his army, a sage over the world.

In its highest aspect the will manifests itself as a self-conscious power, capable of acting far beyond the limits of the corporeal form from which it issues, constituting, so to say, an independent organized spiritual being acting under the guidance of the intelligence of the person from whom it is born. Strange as this assertion may appear, it is nevertheless true, and the now accepted phenomena of "hypnotism" have opened the door to the understanding of such phenomena.[1] An investigation into this subject would bring us within the realm of magic, spiritism, witchcraft, sorcery, etc., etc., which does not belong to our present purpose, and which has been treated in a previous work.[2]

As an evil will is the cause of many diseases, so is a good will a great remedy for curing them. While two fools hypno-tizing each other will produce a mixture of folly, the magic power of the self-conscious benevolent will of an enlightened physician is able to arouse the confidence and restore health in many cases where all the remedies of the pharmacopoeia are of no avail, and the cultivation of this power is therefore of supreme importance, even more so than a knowledge of all the details in regard to the action of drugs. Science and wisdom should be cultivated together, but not the former at the expense of the latter.

---

[1] Any person wishing for information on such points may find it in the literature of spiritism, mediæval witchcraft, in the "Lives of the Saints," etc., etc. Volumes might be filled with such accounts, but phenomena are proofs only to him to whom they occur. A person having no experience of a thing is always at liberty to deny its existence, and it is far easier to call it a "superstition" than to arrive at its understanding by studying secret laws.
[2] "See: *Thomson Jay Hudson.* "The Law of Psychic Phenomena."

Imagination.

"Imagination" means the power of the mind to form *images;* from the shadowy images of a dream up to the corporeal and living images formed by the power of an Adept. This faculty, which was well known to the ancient sages who were in possession of it, is almost entirely ignored by popular medical science, which in spite of its recent discoveries of what is now called "suggestion," does not yet seem to suspect the extent of its power. It is a power whose application cannot be taught to those who do not possess it, and there are very few who have this power developed; for our present generation is of a pre-eminently *adamic* (terrestrial) and impotent kind; leading a dream-life, and being itself composed of dreams, its imagination is as feeble as a dream. The real power of active and effective imagination belongs to the spiritual inner man, who in the vast majority of mankind has not yet awakened to life. Only when men and women have entered into the true life—in other words, when the spirit in them will have become self-conscious—will they be able to possess and to exercise spiritual powers, such as constituted the *Arcana* of Theophrastus Paracelsus, on which there has been so much speculation in modern literature and yet so little really known—the stumbling block and fruitful source of error for so many of our modern *surface* observers.[1]

We do not blame popular medical science for not knowing that which it does not know; but we believe that the presumption of those who figure temporarily as the representatives of science, and who dogmatically pronounce useless and absurd everything which they do not possess, ought not to be encouraged. It is not so very long since recognised science laughed at the rotundity of the earth, and declared officially that no meteors could fall from the sky "because there were no stones in heaven;" denounced the belief in "psychic phenomena" as being a degrading superstition, and ridiculed the idea of building steamboats and telegraphs, etc. These errors originate not from science, but from stupid

---

[1] "Arcanum" means mystery. The key to a mystery is its understanding. The Arcana of Paracelsus were not, as has been asserted by certain "authorities," patent medicines whose composition he kept secret; but they were his knowledge of the means for effecting a cure. He says:—"If there is a stone in the bladder, the *arcanum* is the knife (for performing lithotomy), in (acute) Mania phlebotomy is the arcanum. An arcanum is the entering into a new state, the giving birth to a new thing." *(Lib.* "Paramir.," I. 5, II. 2.) Every plane of existence has its own mysteries and arcane remedies.

ignorance and self-conceit; they are the result of human infirmities, which exist now as in times of old, and can be cured only by the development of a superior power for knowing the truth.

Memory.

The third great power of the spirit manifested in the mind is the power of memory, which is, in fact, the power of man's spirit to visit those places within the sphere of his mind where the impressions of former experiences are preserved, and thus to bring them again within the field of consciousness. Whatever function the physical brain may exercise in using this faculty of the spirit, the brain is no more the memory than the eye the sight; it is merely an instrument for perception, but not the perceiver nor the object of perception, nor the perception itself. To remember a thing is to see its impression or image in the *astral light;* to recollect a thing is to gather together one's own attention at the place where its impression is stored up in the mind, and the power which enables a person to do so is the relation which exists between the creator and his creatures; man having formed a thought or idea, or perceived an image, is able to recollect it, because the impression is his creation—having issued from himself, it is a part of his world.

It depends upon the degree of spiritual power of perception in man, whether he can clearly and vividly see these images in the Astral Light, or whether they appear to him dim, uncertain and indistinct; but in the vast majority of men and women in our present generation this power of perceiving does not penetrate deeper nor rise higher than the Astral Light, while the spiritually developed man can penetrate deeper, and behold the memories of not only his present incarnation, but also those referring to his previous states of existence.

Will, Imagination and Memory are the cause of many diseases and such may be caused by one's perverted use of those faculties, or by being practised upon another. A thought of any kind, be it wicked or virtuous, if rendered strong and substantial by the consent of the will, becomes born in the inner world as an elemental being, which grows by being cultivated, so that it may ultimately obsess its own father and produce visible effects upon the physical frame. The imagination of animals produces change in the colour of their offspring, the imagination of a mother can produce marks upon the child; the recollection of evil events and keeping such memories constantly in the mind gives rise to melancholy, ill temper, and despondency, anger, greed, lust, avarice, etc. All forms of evil will produce not only morbid states of the mind, but also certain definite changes in the physical body; all of which offer a vast field for a science of psychology in the future. An exposition of such a mental science cannot be attempted within the limited space of this work; but there already exists a vast amount of literature on this subject ignored by official science.

V.—ENS DEI.
Diseases arising from eternal Retribution.

A definition of the word "Deus," God, is an impossibility, because it refers to a state beyond the conception of the limited mind. Eckhart says:—"A god of whom I could conceive would not be a god, but a limited creature." We can therefore only say, God is the universal will in its highest aspect as divine love; which is the supreme law and the life of all things. A necessary consequence of the action of divine law is divine justice; because it would be impossible to imagine how one being could be favoured without doing injustice to another, and thus depriving the law of universal divine love of its unity and equality. This divine law of justice, according to which every cause created by a rational being returns with all its effects to its creator, is called in the East the law of *Karma,* and may be translated as the law of Eternal Retribution. H. P. Blavatsky says:—

"*Karma is the unerring law which adjusts effect to cause, on the physical, mental, and spiritual planes of being. As no cause remains without its due effect from greatest to least, from a cosmic disturbance down to the movement of your hand, and as like produces like, Karma is that law which adjusts wisely, intelligently and equitably each effect to its cause, tracing the latter back to its producer.*"[1]

This law of *Karma* is in common parlance called the Will of God; which means the action of divine justice throughout the universe, and it is the cause not only of social evils, distinctions of classes in society, of the unequal distribution of wealth and comfort, good luck and misfortune, but also of defects of character, mental abnormalities and physical diseases.

---

[1] H. P. Blavatsky's "Key to Theosophy," p. 201.

All diseases in fact are effects of the law of *Karma,* the effects of causes, which are all based upon one universal Law; but this is not to be understood as if it meant "fatality," or as if nothing could be done to cure such effects; for *Karma* is also the source of good, and if the patient finds a physician able to cure him, it proves that it was his *Karma* to find him and that he should be cured by him.

"All health and all disease comes from God, who also furnishes the remedy. Each disease is a purgatory, and no physician can effect a cure until the time of that purgatory is over. Ignorant physicians are the devils of that purgatory; but a wise physician a redeeming angel and a servant of God. The physician is a servant of nature; and God is its Lord. Therefore no physician ever performs a cure unless it is the will of God curing the patient through him." ("Paramir.," I., C. iv., 2 and 7.)

To know the theory of a thing is a science, to know how to use it successfully is art.[1] It was the view of the ancient philosophers, and it will also be the view of the physician of the future, that Medicine is not merely a science but a holy art, and that a mere science without true goodness and wisdom is without real value. The practice of medicine must be based not merely upon scientific theories in regard to the laws of that part of nature which is its lowest plane of manifestation, the plane of physical appearances; but at the bottom of all science must be the recognition of eternal Truth itself. Health and disease in man are not determined by physical laws alone, such as govern the lowest orders of being; neither are the laws of Nature created by Nature; *but all natural laws are the outcome of spiritual law acting in Nature,* and in those kingdoms where intelligence plays a part, where the will begins to become free and individual

---

[1] The cause of a certain disease may exist not only in one of these five classes, but in more. For instance, a hæmorrhage of the womb may be caused by mental excitement in connection with a state of weakness of resistance in the tissues of the organs; insanity may be caused by mental, moral or physical circumstances; blindness may be the result of physical causes or of mental excitement; a bodily defect the result of antenatal *Karma,* or of physical causes. In the clockwork of nature all the wheels are connected by one common chain. Therefore not only one of these causes but all of them ought to be known and taken into consideration; but each of the corresponding five methods of treatment contains in itself all the elements for effecting a cure. It is therefore not necessary that a physician should practise all the five methods of treatment; but he should have a thorough knowledge of the method which he has chosen, and be well versed in it and stick to his method; but he should not believe his own method to be the only true one, and reject others of which he knows nothing.

responsibility takes place, a more direct action of divine law becomes manifest. Although therefore a knowledge of the laws of physical nature is extremely useful and necessary, the student of medicine should above all cultivate nobility and spirituality of character, such as is the result of the recognition of the fundamental law of Divine Wisdom, upon which is based all the order and harmony that exists in the world. Thus the practice of medicine has for its foundation not a merely technical side, and is not merely a trade or profession, which anybody may enter who chooses for the purpose of making a living; but it requires for its legitimate object the employment of such faculties as are the result of a development of the higher and nobler elements, the spiritual part in the constitution of man.

IV.
THE FIVE CLASSES OF PHYSICIANS.

THERE being five causes of disease, and as each disease ought to be treated with reference to its cause, there may be distinguished five distinct modes of treatment, which, however, must not be confounded with five different systems such as anyone may choose at his own pleasure, for each of these modes requires the possession of certain distinct natural qualifications, of which the higher are at present only rarely to be found. While the science of the lower methods, such as prescribing drugs, using hot or cold water, or applying any other physical forces, may easily enough be taught to anybody in possession of an ordinary amount of intelligence, the real art of medicine requires higher gifts and talents, which cannot be acquired in any other way than according to the law of spiritual evolution, by the higher development of the inner man. A physician in possession of the powers conveyed by wisdom may also acquire a knowledge of the medical views and technicalities which form the stock in trade of the lower orders of physicians; but a physician of a lower order cannot practise the art of the higher order without becoming initiated into that order by means of the development of the power required for it.

This will make it clear that the quality of the physician himself is of as much importance as the system which he practises, and Paracelsus distinguishes five classes of physicians: the three lower classes seeking for their resources in the material plane; the two higher classes employing remedies belonging to the supersensual plane; but he also says that, owing to the unity of nature, either one of these classes of physicians may accomplish cures in either one of the five fields, and that no physician ought to change around from one system to another; but each ought to stick to that "sect" to which he naturally belongs.

These five classes of physicians he describes as follows:

1. *Naturales;* such as employ physical remedies, acting as opposites; which means, using physical and chemical means, heat against cold, etc., etc. (Allopaths).

2. *Specifici.—Those* who employ certain remedies which experience has shown to act as *specifica* (Empirics, Homœopaths).

3. *Chavacterales.—*Such as employ the powers of the mind;

acting upon the will and imagination of the patient (Mental healers, Mind cure, Mesmerism, &c.).

4. *Spirituales.—Those* who are in possession of spiritual powers, using the magic power of their own will and thought (Magic, Psychometry, Hypnotism, Spiritism, Sorcery).

5. *Fideles.—Those* through whom "miraculous" works are performed in the power of the true faith (Adepts).

To which of these five "sects" or faculties a physician belongs, he ought to be thoroughly versed and experienced in that department, having not merely a superficial but a thorough knowledge of it.

"In whatever faculty one desires to acquire a degree and obtain success, he should, besides regarding the soul and the diseased body of the patient, exert himself to obtain a thorough knowledge of that department, and be taught more by his own intuition and reason than by what the patient can tell him; he ought to be able to recognise the cause and origin of the disease which he treats, and his knowledge ought to be unwavering and not subject to doubts." ("Paramir.," I., Prolog.)

There are, therefore, in each of these classes three grades to be distinguished, namely: (1) those who possess the full requirements of their art; (2) those who have attained only mediocrity; (3) dunces, pretenders and frauds; to which belong the vast array of licensed and unlicensed quacks, such as thrive upon the ignorance and credulity of the people and by means of their poisons and drugs "kill annually more persons than war, famine and the plague combined." But neither of these five classes of physicians should regard their own system as the only true one, and reject the others or consider them useless; for in each is contained the full and perfect power to cure all diseases that come from either of the five causes, and each will be successful if such is the will of the Law.

I.—NATURALES.

To this class belongs the vast army of what is to-day usually termed "regular practitioners," meaning those who move in the old ruts of official medical science, from the more or less progressive physician down to the vendor of drugs. The remedies which they employ belong to the three kingdoms of physical nature, and according to the elements which they represent, may be divided as follows:

1. *Earth.—This* includes all mineral, vegetable, and animal substances that may be required for medical purposes, drugs, herbs, and their preparations, chemical agents, &c.

2. *Water.—To* this belongs the water cure, hot and cold baths," and whatever may be connected with it.

3. *Air.—The* therapeutic results which can be accomplished by means of inhaling certain gases and vapours are at present comparatively little known, except in so far as changes of climate are resorted to for such purposes. The employment of such things as pure air, sunlight, etc., is far too simple to find full appreciation of its value by a generation whose mode of thinking is too complicated to enable them to perceive simple truths, and is therefore considered to belong rather to "hygiene" than to "therapeutics."

4. *Fire.—To* the agents belonging to this class may be counted any kind of energy, heat and cold, sunlight and the actions of its variously coloured rays,[1] physical electricity, mineral magnetism, etc., all of which have thus far received very little attention from modern medicine; while the ancients employed such remedies for the cure of many diseases.[2]

5. *Ether.—The* one element and its action is thus far hardly theoretically admitted by modern science and practically almost unknown. Only very recently a great step of progress in this direction has been made by the discovery of the therapeutic action of the solar ether, and by the employment of an apparatus for the employment of its radiations.[3]

But the sphere of activity for the natural physician is not limited to the extent of the merely physical plane. If he goes a step higher he may employ not only the products of life, but the activity of life itself, in a higher form.[4] The sources from which he receives the physical remedies are the physical products of nature; the sources from which he draws living powers are living organisms. To this department belongs the employment of "animal magnetism;" the transfer of life *(Mumia);* the transplant-

---

[1] The soothing power of blue, the exciting effects of red, the invigorating effects of yellow, etc., deserve a great deal more attention than they receive at present. The reason why the "blue light cure" has caused only a passing excitement, is because it was indiscriminately used and its laws not understood.

[2] "Paracelsus," p. 141.

[3] Professor O. Korschelt in Leipzig invented an instrument for that purpose.

[4] See "Paracelsus," p. 138.

ation of diseases[1] and similar things thoroughly described by Paracelsus, Cornelius Agrippa and others, but which for our present official medical science do not exist.

Even those who employ only gross material principles also employ, without being conscious of it, the higher principles contained therein; for every physical substance, to whatever kingdom in nature it may belong, is an expression of not only one of the four elements, but of all four, and contains all the higher principles. Thus, for instance, it has been shown that the action of certain drugs corresponds to that of the colours which they exhibit in the solar-spectrum;[2] each state of matter also corresponds to a certain state of electric tension; each particle of food proves the presence of the life principle in it by being nutritious; each poisonous drug acting upon the mind, shows thereby that the mind principle therein is in a high state of activity. There is no "dead matter" in the universe; each thing is a representation of a state of consciousness in nature, even if its state of consciousness differs from ours, and is therefore beyond the reach of our recognition; everything is a manifestation of "Mind," even if does not exhibit any intelligent functions, or what we are capable of recognising as such.

For the comprehension of these things, the position adopted by modern natural science is altogether insufficient, and such a philosophical knowledge is required as shall constitute the first pillar in the temple of medicine. There is a vast field still unexplored by modern medical science, and if things which were known to the ancients are not known at present, it is not because such sciences have never existed, but because they have ceased to be understood owing to the materialising tendency of this age.

II.—SPECIFICI.

To this class belong all physicians who under certain circumstances employ certain remedies, of which they know from experience that under similar circumstances similar remedies have proved successful. This system may therefore be called *"Empiricism,"* and it constitutes the greatest part of modern therapeutics; for what little is known to-day of the

---

[1] All forces may become manifest in a threefold form. There are universal, animal and spiritual "magnets"; a physical electricity, an electricity of life, a spiritual electricity, etc., etc.

[2] *Dr Babbitt's* "Principles of Light and Colour."

physiological and therapeutic actions of medicine is on the whole the result of observation, and not of a knowledge of the fundamental laws of nature which cause medicines to act as they do.

Heat is a specific remedy for cold, and moisture for dryness; but even the very opposite remedies often have the same specific effect. Thus, for instance, the pain caused by an inflammation, and the inflammation itself, may be cured by cold as well as by hot applications to the inflamed part; for in one case the walls of the blood vessels contract, diminishing the quantity of the blood rushing to them, while in the other case these vessels dilate, rendering the rush of blood painless and easy. The specific action of chemicals is due to their chemical affinities (harmonies). Thus the invigorating action resulting from the inhalation of fresh air is caused by the affinity which Oxygen has for the Carbon in the blood, and by the life principle of the air upon the life principle in the body. Thus the tubercle-bacilli in the lungs may be destroyed by the specific action of certain gases, which, inhaled, form certain chemical compounds with certain elements contained in these micro-organisms, and thereby cause their destruction.[1] Everything in the universe takes place for a certain reason and has a certain specific action depending on certain conditions. If we know the laws and conditions, experience becomes a science; but where our science is blind, experience can be our guide.

Like knows like. The physical senses only recognise physical things; but all visible things are an expression of soul, and what can we know about the *Soul of Things,* if we do not know that soul which is our own? There can be no motion, where there is no emotion to produce it, either directly or indirectly. All motions are manifestations of energy; energy is a manifestation of consciousness; consciousness is a state of the mind; mind is a vehicle for the manifestation of spirit; spirit is the "Breath" by which the world was *created.*

If the colours of the *Tattwas* and their nature were studied, a new field for medical science would open. It would become possible to explain why a raving maniac kept in a room of blue light will become quieted, and a melancholy person improve in a room filled with red or yellow rags; why a steer will become excited at the sight of red, and a mob infuriated by the sight of

---

[1] F. Hartmann, "Eine neue Heilmethode." W. Friedrich, Leipzig, 1893.

blood. Where the laws in consequence of which certain effects occur are unknown, we can only register the facts. If we recognise a truth by experience we can make use of it, leaving it to sceptical science to arrive at its recognition by hobbling along on its crutches of external observation and inference.

These inferences are often drawn from wrong premises; effects mistaken for causes; drugs administered where the sources of the diseases exist in moral and mental conditions upon which drugs have no effect, etc., etc. The application of specific remedies therefore requires not merely a knowledge that this or that remedy has effected such and such cures, but also a knowledge of the circumstances in which it will produce such effects again. The real *Arcanum* is the understanding of the relation existing between cause and effect. To those shortsighted practitioners who behold in every disease nothing but the manifestation of a purely physical or chemical cause, and to whom "mind," "soul" and "spirit" are terms without meaning or merely physiological functions of unconscious matter, the *Arcana* of such cures will ever remain unknowable mysteries; for they can be known only to those who understand the organization of the inner nature of man. The phenomena caused by life are incomprehensible as long as life is regarded as a product of forms without life; but he who is able to see in every living thing a manifestation of the *One Life* pervading all nature, a function of universal will, has already entered the precincts of that higher science, which cannot be explained by words, if it is not known to the heart.

III.—CHARACTERALES.

A physician of this class is the one whose very presence inspires the patient with confidence in recovery. Consciously or unconsciously such a physician acts upon the two great motive powers in the constitution of the patient, namely his will and his imagination. He who can restore tranquillity of the soul by creating confidence, creates the condition required for the cure of the disturbance of the elements producing discord.

All the processes taking place in the physical body originate in the unconscious or conscious action of the will and the imagination, to which must be added the power of memory; for the existence of former impressions either consciously or unconsciously produces certain states in the imagination, which again determine the direction of will. The average physician often employs these powers unknowingly; a physician of the higher class can employ them intelligently. A sudden strong emotion may in a moment cure a paralytic affection of long standing, a sudden danger arouse the unconscious will. Perhaps in the majority of cases it is not that which the patient takes but that which he imagines that it will cure him, which effects the cure, and without this power of the imagination very few medicines would produce any beneficial results.

To this department belong so-called "hypnotism" and "suggestion," two old things described under new names. Paracelsus says of this action of the spiritual will:

"It is as if one orders another to run and he runs. This takes place by means of the word and through the power of the word; the word being the character." ("Paramir.," Prolog. III.)

So-called "*hypnotism*" is the overcoming of a weak will by a stronger one. The superior will of the physician overcomes the will of the patient and forces it to act in a certain direction. It is an art which is practised continually and constantly by one half of mankind on the other half, from the will power of a general commanding his army down to the unconscious influence unknowingly exercised by one mind over another, without the subject being aware of its source. Evil thoughts originating in one person create corresponding impulses in others, and if the unconscious action of will and the relations which it causes among sympathetic minds were truly known, human freewill and responsibility would perhaps appear in a different light.

Similar to that is what has been called "suggestion," which Paracelsus calls the virtue of the imagination. It is the imagination of one mind overpowering the mind of another and creating therein a corresponding imagination, which is perfectly real to the patient, because it is in reality his own creation produced unconsciously by himself.

"The visible man has his laboratory (the physical body), and the invisible man is working therein. The sun has his rays, which cannot be grasped with the hands, which are nevertheless strong enough to set houses on fire (if gathered by a lens). Imagination in man is like a sun, it acts within his world where-ever it may shine. Man is that which he thinks. If he thinks fire, he is all on fire; if he thinks war, he is warring; by the power of thought alone the imagination becomes a sun." ("De virtute imaginativa," V.)

The imagination becomes strong through the will and the will becomes powerful through imagination. Either of these two is the life of the other, and if they become one and identical, they constitute a living spirit to which nothing inferior offers resistance. In the ignorant and doubtful, in those who do not know their own mind and doubt the result of success, consequently in the majority of experiments carried on for the purpose of gratifying a scientific curiosity or for some other selfish purpose, the will and imagination are not one, but act in two different directions. If we look with one eye to heaven and with the other to the earth, or with one to the restoration of the patient's health and with the other to the profits knowledge or renown we may receive from it ourselves, there is no unity of motive or purpose, and consequently a lack of the principal condition for success. A physician desirous of employing such means should therefore be of such a nobility of character as to be above all selfish considerations, and only intent upon doing his duty according to the commands of divine love.

Only that which comes from the heart goes to the heart; the power that comes from the brain alone has no magic effects unless it becomes united with that which comes from the heart. It resembles the cold and ineffective moonlight, but it becomes a strong power by its union with the sunshine that radiates from the centre of the heart.

"Thus the imagination becomes a spirit, and its vehicle is the body, and in this body are generated the seeds which bear good and evil fruits." ("De virtute imaginativa," III.)

IV.—SPIRITUALES.

Up to this class we have had to deal with forces which are, even if not fully recognized, at least admitted by modern science; but now we are going to speak of the action of a spiritual power, which, being in the conscious possession of only a few persons, is almost entirely unknown. This is the power which the self-conscious spirit exercises over the unintelligent forces in nature, and which comes under the head of "Magic," a term whose meaning is understood only by few.

"Magic"—from *mag,* priest—means the great power of wisdom, an attribute of the self-conscious spirit, holy or devilish according to the purpose to which it is applied. It is therefore a power which does not belong to the terrestrial intellectual man;

but to the spiritual man, and it may even be exercised by the latter without the external man being aware of the source of this power acting in him. For this reason we often see that some remedy proves very efficacious in the hands of one physician and entirely useless in the hands of another equally learned and intellectual. Paracelsus says:

"Such physicians are called *spirituales,* because they command the spirits of herbs and roots, and force them to release the sick whom they have imprisoned. Thus if a judge puts a prisoner in the stocks, the judge is his physician. Having the keys, he may open the locks when he chooses. To this class of physicians belonged Hippocrates and others." ("Paramir.," Prolog. III.)

Such an assertion appears to be incredible only as long as nothing is known about the constitution of matter; but if we call occult science to our aid and realise that all things in the world constitute certain states of one universal consciousness, and that the foundation of all existence is Spirit, it not only becomes comprehensible, but even self-evident, that the self-conscious spirit of a person can move and control the products of nature's imagination according to its own action in them, and we may truly say that in such cases it is the spirit of the physician acting by means of the spirit of the remedies which he employs, and herein is the solution of the secret of the wonderful cures of leprosy, etc., effected by Theophrastus Paracelsus, which have been historically proved, but which are unintelligible if examined from the point of view of material science.

An investigation into this subject would take us within the realm of white and black magic, witchcraft and sorcery, which have received attention already on a previous occasion,[1] and whose further elucidation would be premature and altogether impossible within the limited space of this work.

V.—FIDELES.

The word "fidelity"—from *fido,* to trust—means faith, confidence, conviction arising from the perception of truth ; knowledge, such as results from experience, and the class of physicians here referred to, includes those who, remaining true to their own divine nature, are in possession of divine powers, such as have been attributed to Christ, the apostles and saints.

---

[1] "Magic, white and black." (London, 1893.)

"They restore health by the power of faith; for he who believes in truth becomes healed by its own power." ("Paramir.," I., Prol. 3.)

So-called "faith" is in most cases illusive, and consists merely in an accepted or pretended belief in the correctness of certain opinions or theories. The true faith of the spiritual man is a living spiritual and divine power, resulting from the certitude of the spiritual perception of the eternal law of cause and effect. As we most certainly are convinced that day follows upon the night, and night after day, so the Adept-physician, knowing the spiritual, moral and physical causes of diseases, and appreciating the flow of their evolution and progress, knows the effects created by such causes, and controls the means for their cure. No one can destroy effects caused by the law of divine justice. If he hinders the manifestation of divine law in one way, it will manifest itself in another way, such is the action of divine law in nature; but he who lives in the truth and in whom divine truth becomes manifest, is thereby raised superior to nature, for he enters into that from which nature took its origin. This uplifting and all-saving power is the true faith in man which can cure all diseases.

"There is neither good nor bad luck; but every effect is due to a cause. Each one receives his reward according to the way he walks and acts. God has made all men out of only one substance, and given to all the same power to live, and all human beings are therefore equals in God. The sun and the rain, winter and summer, are the same for everybody; but not everybody looks at the sun with the same eyes. God loves all mankind alike; but not all men love God with the same kind of love. Each of God's children has the same inheritance; but one squanders, while another preserves it. That which God has made equal is rendered unequal by the actions of men. Each man taking his cross upon himself finds therein his reward. Every misfortune is a fortune, because divine goodness gives to everyone that which he most needs for his future development; the suffering begins only when discontent, the result of the non-recognition of eternal law, steps in. The greater the obstacle to combat, the greater will be the victory." ("Philosophia," V.)

The art of medicine has not been instituted for the purpose of defying the laws of God; but for the purpose of aiding in the restoration of the harmony, whose disturbance caused disease, and this restoration takes place through obedience to the law. There is no more a "forgiveness of the sin of disease" than there is a forgiveness of moral sins. The cure takes place by means of a re-entering into harmony with the laws of nature, which after all are the laws of God manifested in the natural realm. Neither is the health restored or sins pardoned for the purpose that man with lessened fear of punishment may go and sin again; but after the effects of the discords are overcome, he obtains again the power to sin, so that he may have a fresh opportunity for overcoming temptation and thus attain mastery over himself during his life upon this earth. He who is master over himself is his own law and not subject to any disharmony, and it is this which Paracelsus expressed in his favourite motto:

"Non sit alterius qui suus esse potest,"

which may be translated, "He who is master over himself belongs to nothing else but himself": for that Self which conquers "self " is God, the Will of Divine Wisdom, the Lord over All.

V.
THE PHYSICIAN OF THE FUTURE.

THERE is no doubt that the average physician of the present age occupies on the whole a much higher position than was occupied by the average physician of the last centuries when the wisdom of the ancients had become a forgotten truth, and modern science was in its infancy. Although there were even during the middle ages physicians of deep insight, and in possession of a profound knowledge of the mysteries of Nature, such as the modern profession may acquire again by slow growth within the next centuries, the popular medicine of these times was a mixture of ignorance and quackery, the remnants of which are still to be found in our days. Of this class of the physicians of those times Paracelsus says:—

"There are a great many among them who have no other object but to satisfy their greed, so that one has to be ashamed to belong to a profession in which so much swindling takes place. They speculate on the ignorance of the people, and he who succeeds in amassing the greatest amount of money by robbing them is looked upon as the leading physician. Mutual love and charity is entirely out of fashion, and the practice of medicine is degraded to the standard of a common trade, in which the only object is to take as much money as one can obtain, and those who have the gift of the gab, and clamour the loudest, succeed best in cheating mankind; for as long as the world is filled with fools, the biggest fool will necessarily be the ruler, if he only succeeds in making himself conspicuous." ("Defensio," V.)

The science of medicine is not to blame for the existence of such a state of things; but it is one of the attributes of human animal nature, and we leave it to the intelligent observer to judge whether this nature has changed a great deal since the time of Paracelsus, or whether there is still an army of quacks, legalized or illegal, who have written the motto *"Mundus vult decipi, ergo decipiatur"* upon their flag. Official science has undoubtedly progressed during this century, but merely intellectual acquisitions do not necessarily make a man wiser; the greatest scoundrels have been men of great intellectuality without spirituality. Wisdom consists in the self-recognition of truth, and there are many who are "ever learning and never able to come to the knowledge of truth."[1]

---

[1] I. Timothy, III., 7.

This spiritual knowledge does not belong to the faculties of men's lower intellectual nature, but to his higher nature alone; and it is therefore of paramount importance that the development of that higher nature should receive more attention than it is receiving at present. A mere improvement in morals or ethics is quite insufficient for that purpose. Morality is the outcome of reasoning; Spirituality is the superior power due to the manifestation of self-consciousness on a higher plane of existence, the illumination of the mind and body of man by the power and light of the spirit filling the soul. When spirituality becomes substantiality in man, then only will his knowledge be of a substantial kind.

This spiritual substantiality, or, in other words, the realization of the highest ideal, is the work of the gradual evolution of mankind; which, as has been said by the ancient alchemists, "may require for its accomplishment thousands of ages; but which can also be accomplished in a moment of time." It is not a product of man's labour, but of the descent of the light of divine truth, the "grace of God" which will come to everyone whenever he is ready to receive it. It is therefore not dependent on anyone's willing or running,[1] but on the action of the spirit of the true divine Self, which is ever striving to become manifest in man.

This interior development is not the consequence of the acquisition of any new theories in regard to the nature of the constitution of man; but takes place through the overcoming of the lower elements in his nature, by means of which his higher nature can become manifest. But in order to induce and enable him to employ his powers intelligently for the purpose of conquering his lower nature, he should learn to know theoretically his own constitution and the nature of the higher powers in him.

These are the elements of that higher science which the physician of the future will have to learn, first theoretically and afterwards in their practical application. Without a spiritual recognition of the fundamental principles of Nature, a seeking from a superficial point of view for a discovery of the mysteries of being is like an unfruitful wandering in a fog. It resembles a search from the periphery of a sphere of unknown extent for a centre whose locality is unknown; while if we have once a correct conception of the situation of that shining centre, its light

---

[1] Romans, IX., *ib.*

will act as a guiding star in our wanderings through the fogs which pervade the realm of phenomena.

Science comes from man; wisdom belongs to God. Of sciences there are many; wisdom is only one. The sciences should be cultivated, but wisdom not be neglected, for without wisdom no true science can exist.

"Nothing (real) is of ourselves; we do not belong to ourselves, but we belong to God. Therefore we must try to find in ourselves that which is of God. It is his and not ours. He has made a body for us, and given us life and wisdom in addition to it, and from these come all things. We should learn to know the object of our existence, and the reason why man has a soul, and what is the will of God that he should do. A study of (terrestrial) man will never reveal the secret and object of his existence, and the reason why he is in the world; but if we once know his creator, we shall also know the qualities of his child; for he who knows the father knows also the son, because the son inherits the (nature of) the father. Each man has the same amount of truth given to him by God; but not everyone recognises that which he has received. He who sleeps knows nothing; he who lives an idle life does not know the power which is in him, and wastes his time. Man is so great and noble that he bears the image of God, and is an heir to the kingdom of God. God is supreme truth, and the devil is supreme falsehood. Falsehood cannot know truth. Therefore if man wants to come into possession of truth, he must know the wisdom which he has received from God. Cleverness belongs to the animal nature, and in regard to many scientific acquisitions animals are superior to man; but the understanding is an awakening which cannot be taught by man. That which one person learns from another is nothing unless there is an awakening. A teacher can put no knowledge into his pupil, he can only aid in the awakening of the knowledge which is already in him." ("De Fundamento Sapientiæ," I.)

Wisdom is the recognition of God. God is the truth, the knowledge of one's own true self is divine wisdom. He who knows his true self knows the divine powers belonging to his God.

"God is Wisdom. He is not a sage or an artist, he is for himself (absolute), but all wisdom and art is born from him; if we know God, we also know his wisdom and art. In God all is one and no pieces. He is the unity, the one in everything. A science dealing only with a piece of the whole, and losing sight of the whole to which it belongs, is abortive and not in possession of truth. He who sees in God nothing but truth and justness sees rightly. All wisdom belongs to God; that which is not of God is a bastard. Therefore the kingdoms of this world fall to pieces, scientific systems change, man-made laws perish, but the recognition of eternal truth is eternal. He who is not a bastard of wisdom, but a true son of the father, is in possession of wisdom. This wisdom is that we live in regard to each other as the angels live, and if we live like the angels they will become our own self, so that nothing divides us from them but the physical form, and as all wisdom and art is with the angels, so it will be with us. The angels are the powers through which the will of God is executed. If the will of God is executed through us, we shall be his angels ourselves. The will of God cannot be performed through us unless we are ourselves after the will of God. A fool or a dunce or a greedy person is not after the will of God; how could that will be executed through him? It is of little use to believe that Solomon was wise, if we are not wise ourselves. We are not born for the purpose of living in ignorance, but that we should be like the father, and that the father may recognise himself in the son. We are to be lords over nature, and not nature be lord over us. This is spoken of the angelic man *(Buddhi)* in whom we shall live and through whom we shall see that all our doing and leaving undone, all our wisdom and art is of God." ("De Fundamento Sapientiæ," II.)

All this, however, will be incomprehensible and be condemned as nonsense by what Paracelsus justly calls the "scientific fool," because the wisdom of which he speaks is not the intellect of the terrestrial, but the understanding of the celestial mind. It is that rare power of spiritual self-knowledge which cannot be taught in words, but which is the result of an interior unfolding of the faculties of the soul. The true physician is not made by schools of learning; he becomes one through the light of divine wisdom itself.

"Man has two understandings; the angelic and the animal power of reason. Angelic understanding is eternal; it is of God and remains in God. The animal intellect also originates from God and within ourselves; but it is not eternal; for the animal body dies and its reason dies with it. No animal faculty remains after death; but death is only a dying of that which is animal and not of that which is eternal." ("De Fundamento Sapientiæ," II.)

The term "wisdom" comes from *vid,* to see, and *dôm,* a judgment; it therefore refers to that which is seen and understood, but not to opinions or theories derived from inference, or based on the assertion of others. It is not the product of observation and speculation, memory or calculation, but is the result of interior growth, and all growth comes from nourishment. As the intellect is enlarged by intellectual acquirements, so divine wisdom in man grows by absorbing the nutriment which it receives from the light of Divine Wisdom.

"Everything is of the nature of that from which it is born. The animal in man is nourished by animal food, the angel in him by the food of the angels. The animal spirit belongs to the animal mind, and in the animal mind of man are contained all the potentialities which are separately possessed by the different classes of animals. You may develop in a man the character of a dog, a monkey, a snake, or of any other animal; for man in his animal nature is nothing more than an animal and the animals are his teachers and surpass him in many ways; the birds in singing, the fish in swimming, etc. He who knows many animal arts is for all that not more than an animal or a menagerie of different animals; his virtues, no less than his vices, belong to his animal nature. Whether he possesses the fidelity of a dog, the matrimonial affection of a dove, the mildness of a sheep, the cleverness of a fox, the skill of a beaver, the brutality of an ox, the voracity of a bear, the greed of a wolf, etc., all this belongs to his animal nature; but there is a higher nature of an angelic character in him, such as the animals do not possess, and this angelic being requires that nutriment which comes from above and corresponds to its nature. From the hidden animal spirit in nature grows the animal intellect; from the mysterious action of the angelic spirit grows the super-terrestrial man; for man has a father who is eternal and for him he shall live. This father has placed him in an animal body, not that he should only dwell and remain therein, but that he should by living in it overcome it." ("De Fundam. Sap.," III.)

The animal mind, filled with self-conceit and pride in its evanescent possessions, is entirely incapable of conceiving the nature of the angelic mind, or of forming an idea of the extent of its powers; neither can it grasp the true meaning of a language that deals with the things that belong to that higher nature and believes it to be but delusions and dreams.

"The vanity of the learned does not come from heaven, but they learn it from each other and upon this basis they build their church." ("De Fund. Sap." Fragm.)

"Faith without works is dead," and as we are speaking of spiritual things, the "work" which the true faith requires is of a spiritual character, meaning spiritual action, growth and development. A faith without substantiality is merely a dream; a science without true knowledge is an illusion; a merely senti-mental desire without any active exercise for the attainment of truth is useless. A person living in such dreams and fancies about ideals which he never attempts to realise, dreams only of treasures which he does not possess. He is like a person wasting his life in studying the map of a country in which he might travel, but never making a start. A merely ideal religion, which is never realized and does not substantially nourish the soul, is only imaginary and serves but to amuse; a science which is not practically employed remains an unfruitful theory, serving at best for the gratification of animal curiosity.

The work which *Faith* requires is a continual *Self-Sacrifice,* which means a continual striving to overcome the animal and selfish nature, and this victory of the high over the low is not accomplished by that which is low, but can only take place through the power of divine *Love,* which means the recognition of the higher nature in man and its practical application in daily life. This is the kind of love of which the great mystic of the 17th century, John Scheffler, speaks when he says:

"Faith without love aye makes the greatest roar and din,
The cask sounds loudest when there is nought within."

Without this practical application all virtues are only dreams and cannot grow into substantial powers, nor be employed as such.

Shakespeare says:

"It is a good divine that follows his own instructions."—"Merchant of Venice.")

but such characters are at the present time very rare, for the world now lives only in dreams. "There are "divines" knowing nothing of any divinity; medical practitioners knowing nothing about medicine; "anthropologists" knowing nothing about the nature of man; lawyers knowing nothing of justice; "humanitarians" beggaring their employees; "christians" to whom Christ is unknown. In every sphere of life the external is mistaken for the internal, the illusion for the reality, while the reality remains unrealized and therefore unknown.

A superficial science can concern itself only with superficial causes and effects, however deeply it may enter into the details of such superficialities. The mysterious powers in nature, the intelligent forces in man, are at present almost entirely unknown, and *there is no other way of penetrating into the deeper secrets of nature except by the development of the higher nature of man.*

In ancient times the physician was considered sacred and belonged to the priesthood, not to a priesthood appointed only by man, but to a strong and real priesthood anointed by God. The physician of the future will be again a king and a priest; for only he who is not merely nominally but truly divine can be in possession of divine powers. In him the triangular pyramid consisting of science, religion and art will culminate in one point, called Self-knowledge or Divine Wisdom, where man himself becomes identified with that superior light and intelligence—his true self—of whose ray his personality is a vehicle, image and symbol.

There is a long and weary road to be travelled yet before mankind will arrive at this summit of perfection, and the goal is so far away that only few are able to see it, while to many it will be an apparently unrealisable ideal, and, like a mountain peak lost in the clouds, inconceivable; but the ideal exists and the clouds that hinder us from seeing it are our own errors and misconceptions; it remains with ourselves to clear them away.

We ourselves, by the power of so much of the perception of truth as we have already received and which has become our own, have it within our reach to overcome the darkness and open our minds to the influence of the light. But the light itself we cannot create or manufacture; it is not the product of our calculations, influences and theories. The truth is self-existent, eternal; it may be perceived, but it cannot be made.

The reason why so few can realise the meaning of the term "self-knowledge," is that the knowledge obtained in our schools is exclusively of an artificial kind. We read that which other men have believed and known and we imagine we know it. We fill our minds with the thoughts of others and find little time to think for ourselves. We seek to arrive at a conviction of the existence of this or that object by means of arguments and inferences, while we refuse to open our eyes and to see ourselves the very thing about whose existence we argue. Thus from a theosophical point of view we should appear to a higher being like a nation of people with closed eyes arguing about the existence of the sun and unable or unwilling to look at it for ourselves.

There is only one way to arrive at real self-knowledge, and this is *Experience*. By external experience we attain knowledge of external circumstances; by experiencing internal powers we attain internal knowledge of them. *To know* in reality means *to be*. By becoming material we learn the laws ruling in matter; by becoming spiritual we learn the laws of the spirit; our will is free to guide us in either direction. We cannot know truth in any other way than by becoming true, nor wisdom except by becoming wise. We can know any external or internal power, be it heat or light, love or justice, only by the effects which we experience from its action upon or within our own self.

Man's life in his present condition resembles a dream, and the dreams of humanity as a whole, no less than those of the individual, repeat themselves over and over again. They come and go and come again, appearing perhaps in changed forms, like clouds floating upon the sky and assuming different shapes, but representing the old, ever-returning illusions. While above them, unseen and unknown, shines the sunlight of eternal, unchanging truth, whose presence may be felt like the warm rays of the sun penetrating the clouds, but which to be known requires to be seen. The temple of nature is open to everyone who is able to enter; its light is free to everyone who is able to see; everything is a manifestation of truth, but it requires the presence of truth in ourselves to enable us to perceive it. That which hinders us from entering the temple of nature, from seeing the light and perceiving the truth, are the shadows which we ourselves have created. The real object of the lights kindled by science is not to reveal the truth—which requires no artificial light to be seen, and whose own light is quite sufficient for that purpose—but to destroy the fogs which hinder us from seeing the truth. No one would think of examining the sun by the light of a candle; but the candle-light may guide us through the dark passages of the labyrinth of matter to the door which opens upon the surface, where after the daylight is seen, artificial help is no longer required. But as in seeking our way through a tunnel the best guide is the light that shines from afar through the entrance, so a perception of truth in the heart is the only reliable guiding star in the labyrinth of ever-changing illusions.

All the scientific lights in which this light of eternal truth is not reflected, however radiant they may be, are only so many will-o'-the-wisps misleading the wanderer. All scientific theories and hypotheses based upon a non-recognition of the inner constitution of man and denying his super-terrestrial origin are founded on a misconception of truth. Such opinions are continually subject to change, and no new theory of that kind exists at present which has not existed in some similar shape before. But the truth itself is independent of these opinions, it has always existed and there have always been some who were capable of recognising it, and others who, unwilling or unable to see it, based their knowledge upon misconceptions and superstitious beliefs founded upon other men's assertions.

Modern medical science, with all its modern aids and paraphernalia, has only succeeded in working itself up to a more detailed knowledge of some less important phenomena in the kingdom of matter; while a great number of far more important things that were known to the ancients have been forgotten. As to the power of the soul over the body, tremendous as it is, almost nothing is known; because the souls of those who live entirely in the kingdom of speculations evolved by their brain, are asleep and unconscious. An unconscious soul can no more exert any power than an unconscious body; its motions can at best be instinctive, because deprived of the light of intelligence. It is far more important to the progress of real science that the soul of man should awaken to a recognition of its own higher nature, than that the treasures of a science dealing with the illusions of life should be enriched by any new theories in which there is no recognition of the one foundation of truth. All that any sound theory or any reliable hook can possibly do, is to displace a false theory which prevents man from seeing correctly; but the truth itself can be exhibited or revealed by no man and no theory, it can be seen only by the eye of the true understanding, when it reveals itself in its own light.

It has been said that it is not within the reach of science to enter the realm of noumena which underlie all phenomena and are their cause of manifestation; but without a recognition of the *noumenoh* from which all phenomena spring, a true science (from *scio,* to know) will be as impossible as a system of mathematics with an ignoring of the existence of the number *one* from which all other numbers take their origin and without which no number exists. The soul in us is fundamentally identical with the One from which all phenomena originate. The soul which *is* can know that which is, while that in us which merely *appears* to be belongs to and deals with the realm of appearances.

The acquisition of this higher science therefore requires less an exertion of the speculative faculties of the brain than an awakening of the soul; is advanced less by an evolution of thoughts of various kinds than by the development of the inner man who is doing the thinking and causing the evolution of thoughts, for if that which is able to know in man does not know its own self, all the thoughts and ideas inhabiting the sphere of man's mind will have no legitimate owner, but exist there merely as the reflections of the thoughts of other men, gathered around an illusion called the personal self.

The more the mind analyses a thing and enters into its minor details the easier does it lose sight of the whole; the more man's attention is divided into many parts, the more will he step out of his own unity and become complicated himself. Only a great and strong spirit can remain dwelling within its own self-consciousness, and, like the sun, which shines into many things without becoming absorbed by them, looks into the minor details of phenomena without losing sight of the truth which includes the whole. The most simple truths are usually the ones which are the most difficult to be grasped by the learned, because the perception of a simple truth requires a simple mind. In the kaleidoscope of ever-varying phenomena the underlying truth cannot be seen upon the surface. As the intellect becomes more and more immersed in matter, the eye of the spirit becomes closed; truths which in times of old were self-evident have now been forgotten, and even the meaning of the terms signifying spiritual powers has become lost in proportion as mankind has ceased to exercise these powers. Owing to the conceit of our age of selfishness, which seeks to drag spiritual truths down to the scientific conception of a narrow-sighted animal rationalism, instead of rising up to their level, the character of modern popular science is shown in the amount of cleverness with which illusory self-interests are protected; "faith," the all-saving power of spiritual knowledge, is believed to be superstition; "benevolence" folly, "love" means selfish desires, "hope" is now greed, "life" the creation of a mechanical process, "soul" a term without Meaning, "spirit " a nonentity, "matter" a thing of which nothing is known, etc.

All this has been written to no purpose, if we have not succeeded in making it clear that real progress in the knowledge of human nature is only possible by means of a higher development of the inner nature of the physician himself. No one can attain any real knowledge of man's higher state unless he attains to it himself by purity of motive and nobility of character. Only by recognising his body as a vehicle for the development and manifestation of a superior intelligence will he be able to realise the meaning of the words of Carlyle, who tells us that man in his innermost nature is a divine being, and that whoever puts his hand upon a human form touches heaven.

Wisdom must be the Master, science the servant. Science is the handmaid of wisdom; wisdom the queen. Science is a product of man's imagination; wisdom the spiritual recognition of truth. Material science is a product of the essentially selfish desire to know; wisdom recognises no separation of interests, it is the self-recognition of universal and eternal truth in man. Science, guided by wisdom, can enter into the deepest mysteries of universal being by entering into the Unity of the All; but if science attempts to employ wisdom for the gratification of curiosity or other selfish ends, it is in opposition to wisdom and becomes folly. Therefore a favourite motto of the ancient Rosicrucians (of which Theophrastus Paracelsus was one), but which is understood by only a few, said: "*I know nothing, I desire nothing, I love nothing, I enjoy nothing in heaven or upon the earth but Jesus Christ and him crucified.*" This did not mean that they resolved to remain ignorant, or to lose themselves in pious reveries and dreams of past events, for Paracelsus also said: "God does not desire us to be ignorant blockheads and stupid fools"—but it meant that they had given up the whole of the illusion of self with all its necessarily illusive knowledge, desires, attractions and joys, and entered into the consciousness of that divine intelligence which during this earth-life is as it were crucified in man, and by entering into the higher spiritual state they had become one with Him, who is Himself the Truth in themselves and the source of all knowledge in heaven and upon the earth.

Forever the truth shines in the eternal kingdom of Light but the world of mind wherein our terrestrial nature moves, has its astrological laws, comparable to those that rule in the visible world and are known to astronomy. As the earth recedes from the sun in winter time and approaches it in the summer, so the spiritual evolution of man has its periods of spiritual enlightenment and of mental darkness, and there are little periods within the large periods, as here are days and nights in the year. Man, whether considered as representing humanity as a whole, a nation a people, a family, or an individual, resembles a planet revolving around its own axis between the two poles of birth and decay. That which is uppermost turns down and that which is below rises again to the surface. Truths disappear and are forgotten only to reappear again embodied in new and perhaps improved forms. Civilizations, systems of philosophy, religion and science come and go and come again, the absurdities of fashion that have been the pride of our parents and were laughed at by us become again the objects of admiration for our children, and the forgotten wisdom of the past will be again the wisdom of future generations. Thus the wheel would ever revolve in a circle, there would be no progress and no object of life, if the presence of the eternal sun of Divine Wisdom acting upon the centre of the wheel did not attract it towards itself and thus in the course of ages gradually transform the circular motion into a spiral gyration. At every turn of the great wheel its axis moves imperceptibly a little nearer to the source of all Life, although every period of evolution begins again at the foot of the ladder. The ladder upon which we are climbing stands perhaps upon a little higher ground than the one upon which our ancestors climbed, or which we climbed ourselves during previous incarnations; but there are many steps upon it which our forefathers have ascended and which we shall have to reach. The science of medicine forms no exception to this general rule, and we may safely assert that *the system of medicine of Theophrastus Paracelsus, in its recognition of fundamental laws of nature is of such a high character that it will be for the medical science of the coming centuries to grow up to its understanding,* nor will this advance in science be possible without a corresponding development, and this development will be inaugurated by a correct conception of the constitution of man.

While modern medical science has become degraded almost into a mere trade, flourishing under the protection of its self-interests which it receives from Governments, the medicine of the ancients was a holy art, requiring no artificial protection, because, standing upon its own merit, it rested upon its own success. The adept-physicians of the past performed cures which whenever exceptionally performed at present are called miraculous, and their possibility is denied by the majority of the learned; because they are not in possession of the spiritual powers required for their accomplishment, and consequently cannot conceive of the existence of such powers. Where is the physician of the present day who knows the extent of the power of the spiritually-awakened will acting at a distance of thousands of miles, or the power which human thought can exercise over the imagination of nature? Where is the professor of science who can consciously transfer his soul to a distant place by the power of thought and act there as if he were bodily present? The proof that these things have been done and are done even now is established as much as any other fact resting upon observation and logic; nevertheless it is popularly considered "scientific" to deny such facts and to treat the theory which explains them with contempt. The finer forces of nature are so thoroughly unknown to gross material minds that to mention their existence raises a roar of merriment among those who, being ignorant of the extent of the powers hidden in the constitution of man, require a sledge-hammer to kill a fly and a cannon to shoot at a sparrow.

While the eyes of material science are directed downwards, seeking within the bowels of matter and finding only perishing treasures, the sentimental idealist revels in dreams without substance. Being habituated to objective contemplation, the idealist obtains nothing real; for keeping distant from the object of his research for the purpose of seeing it objectively, he prevents himself from becoming identified with that object, and he cannot have any self-knowledge of that which he is not himself. Neither can the materialist who denies the existence of Spirit in the universe have any real knowledge, for he ignores that which alone is real and deals only with the relations existing between phenomena which the unknown spirit produces. Real knowledge such as is the product not of mere knowing, but of *becoming,* ought to be the basis of all true science. This it is which constitutes that *Theosophia or Self-recognition of Truth,* which will be the guiding star of the physician in the future as it has been in the past.

Made in the USA
Middletown, DE
16 February 2020